Recollections
of
My Slavery Days

William Henry Singleton in his Grand Army of the Republic uniform, Peekskill, New York, ca. 1920. Photograph courtesy of Leroy Fitch, New Haven, Connecticut.

Recollections
of
My Slavery Days

William Henry Singleton

Introduction and Annotations
by
Katherine Mellen Charron and David S. Cecelski

Division of Archives and History
North Carolina Department of Cultural Resources
Raleigh
1999

*Published with special assistance
from Tryon Palace Historic Sites & Gardens*

To Leroy Fitch

and

*In memory of Mary and Solange,
Vera and Irene*

Contents

List of Maps and Illustrations ix

Foreword xi

Preface xiii

Introduction 1

Recollections of My Slavery Days 29

Appendix A: Chronology 55

Appendix B: Genealogy 63

Notes 67

Works Cited 105

Index 115

Maps and Illustrations

William Henry Singleton . . . . Frontispiece

Map of Garbacon Creek area 4

Detail of Colton Map (1861) 6

List of John S. Nelson's slaves 16

Slave lots #1 and #2 17

Following Page 54

William Henry Singleton

Map of New Bern

Gaston House Hotel

African American volunteers to the Union army

Ambrose E. Burnside

Charles Slover House

John Wright Stanly House

John Gray Foster

James Chaplin Beecher

African American troops liberating slaves

Battle of Olustee

James Walker Hood

Lulu W. Singleton

William Henry Singleton's tombstone

Foreword

One of the most neglected aspects of North Carolina history is the active and heroic role that the state's African Americans played in securing their freedom from slavery. More than six decades ago, W. E. B. Du Bois, a leading black intellectual, declared what historians generally have only recently acknowledged: that slaves during the American Civil War were not merely the passive recipients of liberty bestowed upon them by the Emancipation Proclamation and the invasion of white Union troops into the Confederate states. Rather, as North Carolina's enslaved population learned of the Federal army's occupation of eastern portions of the Tar Heel State, thousands of them took their fate into their own hands and broke the chains of bondage by fleeing to freedom within Union lines. From there they continued to struggle to secure new lives for themselves and their loved ones. Many of them joined the U.S. Army as members of the famed African Brigade and fought to maintain their liberty and to win freedom for their families and friends still enslaved.

One such black North Carolinian was William Henry Singleton, a Craven County slave born about 1843, who fled from his master, served as a soldier in the Union army, and migrated north after the Civil War. In his autobiography, *Recollections of My Slavery Days*, first published in 1922, Singleton recounted his years as a slave, his flight to freedom, and his service in the African Brigade. For many years this dramatic personal account remained dormant and unnoticed by historians. Now, however, the Historical Publications Section is extremely pleased to publish a new, annotated edition of this important but long-overlooked work.

The two scholars responsible for the renaissance of the Singleton autobiography are native North Carolinians Katherine Mellen Charron and David S. Cecelski. Ms. Charron, a doctoral student at Yale University, began her investigation of Singleton as part of a research project sponsored by Tryon Palace Historic Sites & Gardens, and funded by the Tryon Palace Council of Friends, Inc., with grant assistance provided by the Kellenberger Historical Foundation. Her pursuit of her subject led to her exploration of a significant number of sources, some of them obscure, and uncovered much new information about Singleton's life and career. The idea of investigating, verifying, and republishing the former slave's recollections originated with Dr. Cecelski, an independent scholar who holds a doctorate from Harvard University and has written extensively about the state's history, particularly of its African American population. His many publications include *Along Freedom Road: Hyde County, North Carolina, and the Fate of Black Schools in the South*, published by the University of North Carolina Press in 1994. Through their relentless efforts in researching and annotating *Recollections of My Slavery Days*, Ms. Charron and Dr. Cecelski have made a substantial contribution to North Carolina historiography. At the Historical Publications Section, they were assisted by editors Lang Baradell, who saw the book through press, and Lisa D. Bailey, who applied her proofreading skills to the project.

Joe A. Mobley, *Administrator*
Historical Publications Section

Preface

We have been following William Henry Singleton's path for several years. This journey has taken us to archives in five states, to the North Carolina coastal village where he was a slave, and to the New England neighborhoods where he lived as a free man. Along the way there have been unforeseen twists and turns, back-road detours, and many points where we thought we had exhausted Singleton's trail. Time and again, when we least expected it, a new piece of evidence emerged that gave entirely new meaning to the fragments of the documentary record we had already collected. At times, what we learned about Singleton's life and his *Recollections* seemed to have as much to do with fate as with the rigors of our historical scholarship.

We first located William Henry Singleton's slave narrative in the New York Public Library while searching for manuscripts on maritime life in the antebellum South. We were surprised to discover that Singleton had been a slave on a Craven County, North Carolina, plantation only a few miles from the rural neighborhood where one of us, David Cecelski, grew up and continues to live much of the year. The bucolic landscape, place names, and family backgrounds described by Singleton evoked a striking sense of familiarity even at first reading. Upon closer study, Singleton's narrative presented a host of complex puzzles whose difficulty might have shaken our resolve had we not shared in and trusted his intimate knowledge of that place. We carried this trust as we visited county courthouses, archives, and museum collections in North Carolina to investigate Singleton's years as a slave.

Next Singleton led us to New Haven, Connecticut, where he settled after the Civil War. It was at this same time that our volume's other editor, Katherine Mellen Charron, prepared to begin graduate study in history at Yale University. Moving to New Haven allowed her to become acquainted with the central institutions of Singleton's postwar life: his neighborhood, church, lodge, and chapter of the Grand Army of the Republic. Discovering his grave in the veterans' section of Evergreen Cemetery on a crisp and sunny morning last spring remains a most memorable moment on this journey to chronicle Singleton's life.

More importantly, it was in New Haven, by a remarkable happenstance, that we had the honor to meet Singleton's only living grandson, Leroy Fitch, himself a lifelong resident of that city. Like his grandfather, Mr. Fitch is a prominent member of New Haven's African American community and his local Masonic lodge. Twenty-three years old when Singleton died in 1938, he generously shared with us both his reminiscences and several extraordinary photographs of his grandfather. Mr. Fitch recalled that Singleton took special delight in speaking to children at the neighborhood schools on Memorial Day. He also introduced us to Charles Twyman, New Haven's first African American principal, who remembered gathering often with a group of neighborhood boys on Singleton's front porch and listening to the elderly veteran describe the Civil War and his meeting with President Lincoln. Mr. Twyman emphasized that he and his friends viewed their distinguished neighbor as a living hero. "Mr. Singleton always wore his hat with pride and at a right angle," Twyman told us, "and he always walked with purpose through the world."

Finally, Mr. Fitch directed us to the family of his brother, Milton Fitch Sr., another grandson, who migrated back to North

Carolina after World War II. Milton Fitch Sr. died a few years ago, but was well-known as a state coordinator for the Southern Christian Leadership Conference during the 1960s. In fact, Dr. Cecelski had interviewed Milton Fitch Sr. for his first book, *Along Freedom Road*, shortly before we located Singleton's narrative in New York. Mr. Fitch's son, Milton "Toby" Fitch Jr., is currently a state representative from Wilson, North Carolina. In Representative Fitch's life and in that of his father we discovered a notable continuity in the family's commitment to the black freedom struggle across the generations. And with the trail leading back to North Carolina, Singleton's story seemed to have come full circle.

* * *

We could not have completed this study of Singleton's life and *Recollections* without the generous support of the Kellenberger Foundation, the Friends of Tryon Palace, and the Tryon Palace Historic Sites and Gardens in New Bern, North Carolina. Sponsoring our work on *Recollections* is the first effort of a broader, long-term commitment by Tryon Palace to represent an African American past that has too frequently been ignored at historic sites and museums in North Carolina and elsewhere in the South. We are indebted to the staff of Tryon Palace, particularly Kay Williams and Nelson McDaniel, both of whom immediately recognized the importance of Singleton's narrative. Special thanks must be reserved for Peter Sandbeck, a Tryon Palace historian who knows Craven County and New Bern better than anyone. He shared his knowledge with us and tirelessly tracked down many local records.
    Our gratitude extends to the archivists, curators, and librarians who assisted us in following Singleton's path and

evaluating the factors that most influenced his life. We would especially like to thank Francis Skelton of the Whitney Library at the New Haven Colony Historical Society; W. D. Barry of the Maine Historical Society; Barbara Zimmer of the Field Library in Peekskill, New York; Alice Cotton and Bob Anthony of the North Carolina Collection and Dick Schrader of the Southern Historical Collection at the University of North Carolina at Chapel Hill; Bill Erwin of the Special Collections Department at Duke University; and John Curran of the Peekskill Museum. We are also indebted to the Reverend Vernon Tyson for his insightful comments on Methodist Church history, and to Dollie C. Carraway of South River, North Carolina, for welcoming us into her home and sharing with us a good deal of local knowledge to which only a lifelong resident would be privy. Our understanding of the Craven County Nelsons would have remained incomplete without her stellar genealogical study. In addition, Laurel Vlock, who published a novel based on Singleton's narrative thirty years ago, reminisced about Lulu Singleton Fitch's family in New Haven and was instrumental in connecting us to Leroy Fitch. It goes without saying that our appreciation to Mr. Fitch and Charles Twyman is boundless.

We are likewise deeply obliged to Tim Tyson and Steve Kantrowitz of the University of Wisconsin at Madison; Glenda Gilmore of Yale University; and Paige Raibmon of Simon Fraser University in Vancouver. Their constant friendship and encouragement are among our most precious treasures. Tim Tyson has been a mentor, a professional collaborator, and a brother in the spirit. His profound insight into the higher purposes of scholarly research and writing continues to inspire us in all of our endeavors. Glenda Gilmore, home girl and role model, led the tour through Singleton's New Haven. She also provided thoughtful counsel by underscoring the primacy of "place" as it informs the process of historical inquiry. With his contagious enthusiasm and extensive knowledge of the antebellum South, Steve Kantrowitz played a crucial role in helping us to solve the more perplexing puzzles of Singleton's narrative. And Paige Raibmon, now so far away, was always there when we needed her. Her brilliant criticism and abiding confidence have meant the world to us.

Heartfelt thanks must go to Perri Morgan, Hope Tyson, and Sam Tyson for their many kindnesses while we were editing this book. The friendship of Miles Johnson, a fellow New Haven hot chocolate connoisseur, has also meant much to us. The love and support of Laura Hanson, Vera Cecelski, and Guy Cecelski make even the most difficult journeys worthwhile. And the steady faith of Pat Nixon remains unsurpassed. Her invincible optimism shines as a beacon, illuminating the most distant shores of possibility.

Finally, our greatest debt is to George Stevenson, the private manuscript archivist at the North Carolina State Archives in Raleigh. We could not have undertaken this project without his guidance or finished this book without his help. Mr. Stevenson showed us far more than the fine points of unraveling historical dilemmas with wills, deeds, and estate records. He taught us that the study of history must ultimately be guided by a knowledge of the human heart. That is, no doubt, why he is so good at it.

Katherine Mellen Charron
and David S. Cecelski

Introduction

In September 1938, William Henry Singleton left his home in New Haven, Connecticut, and joined 118 fellow veterans of the Civil War at the seventy-second Grand Army of the Republic (G.A.R.) encampment in Des Moines, Iowa. His wife, Mary, doubted the wisdom of undertaking such a long trip; her ninety-five-year-old husband's vision was severely impaired, and he suffered from heart trouble. She herself had not been born until eleven years after Appomattox and may not have understood the compelling circumstances that drew her husband halfway across America. By this time, however, she would have been well acquainted with his determination to participate in such patriotic celebrations. Given his declining health and his unwavering resolve to attend, Mrs. Singleton had no choice but to accompany her husband to the G.A.R. reunion. Singleton was especially determined to participate in the parade of Union veterans on the afternoon of September 7. The thermometer had climbed to a sweltering ninety degrees by the time G.A.R. commander in chief O. H. Mennet surveyed his aged troops before beginning the procession through the city's streets. Despite the heat and their advanced age, thirty-eight veterans elected to walk the entire fifteen blocks. William Henry Singleton was one of them, and the march must have filled him with great pride. Born in bondage, he had been among the first of the former slaves to enlist in the Union army in New Bern, North Carolina. During the war, he had fought for his freedom alongside thousands of other black men, mostly liberated slaves, in what was known as the "African Brigade."

The young Singleton had proven himself willing to give his life for his country. He believed that his country would, in turn, be morally obligated to grant him first-class citizenship. Now, seventy-five years later, the elderly grandfather sought to remind his fellow citizens of this unfulfilled promise to the African American veterans of the Civil War. He joined the parade knowing that his wartime service stood as a lasting testament to all of his grandchildren: his fighting as a soldier in the Thirty-fifth United States Colored Troops (U.S.C.T.) directly linked his freedom to theirs. The G.A.R. encampment, as it turned out, was the last time that Singleton would stand as a witness to his people's struggle for freedom. Only hours after the parade, having accomplished what he set out to do, William Henry Singleton suffered a heart attack and died.[1]

Perhaps there were some in Iowa that day who knew of Singleton and his accomplishments. In 1922, sixteen years before his death, Singleton recorded the events of his life in *Recollections of My Slavery Days*, a compelling account of a long and remarkable journey from slavery to freedom in the American South. In this memoir Singleton highlights his days as a slave in antebellum North Carolina, his escape to Union-occupied territory during the Civil War, and the early portion of his wartime service, before concluding with a brief sketch of his life following 1865. At the time he published *Recollections*, Singleton was a respected member of the community in Peekskill, New York, where his life story first appeared in serial form in the *Highland Democrat*, a local weekly newspaper.[2] Later, the publisher of the *Highland Democrat* issued a pamphlet-sized version of the complete work. Released in a limited edition, *Recollections* was never widely distributed and has remained in obscurity for several generations. Even the editors of the most authoritative scholarly surveys of the slave narratives do not seem to have been aware of Singleton's autobiography. Copies of the work are exceedingly rare; only two of the original editions are known to have survived, one housed at the New York Public Library, the other at the Peekskill Museum.

* * *

Born in New Bern, North Carolina, in or around 1843, William Henry Singleton grew up on the John Handcock Nelson plantation at Garbacon Creek, in the most remote corner of Craven County. Garbacon Creek is a small tributary of the Neuse River, at that point a fertile estuary nearly three miles wide, and was a good forty miles from the county seat at New Bern. A primarily agricultural county on the Coastal Plain, Craven had 14,709 residents—half of whom were African American—in 1850.[3] Only a dozen small planters and several hundred of their slaves lived in the immediate vicinity of John H. Nelson, whose neighborhood was loosely defined as being between two brackish bays, Adams Creek and South River.

A vast longleaf pine forest separated the Nelson plantation from New Bern to the west, a large stretch of it settled by free black landholders who received their freedom and land in exchange for military service in the Revolutionary War. Many intermarried with Native American survivors of the Tuscarora War of 1711-1713, and nineteenth-century residents of this predominantly black territory referred to it as "Little Egypt."[4] To the south of Garbacon Creek lay the Open Ground pocosin, a vast raised bog dominating a twenty-mile-wide peninsula that separates the Lower Neuse from the Atlantic. A broad swamp forest extended beyond Garbacon Creek to the east, fading fifteen miles farther at Turnagain Bay into a salt marsh, most of it uninhabitable to this day.

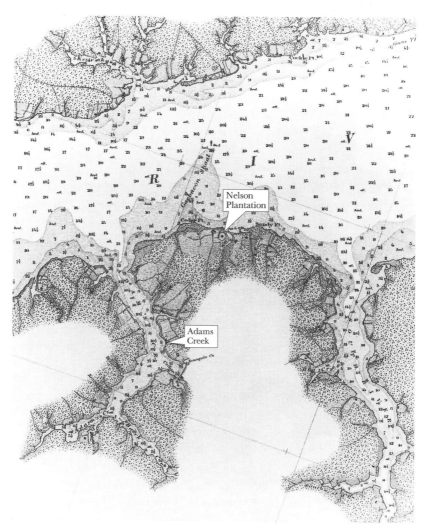

Map of Garbacon Creek area, Craven County. U.S. Coast Survey, Neuse River, N.C., 1874. Map from the files of the Division of Archives and History.

John H. Nelson's ancestors could scarcely have chosen a more inhospitable location to settle. Vulnerable to hurricanes in the autumn and the chilly northeasterly winds of winter, the Neuse's southern shores were also sheltered from the cool southwesterly breezes that blow off the Atlantic in the summer, making that season rife with mosquitoes, ticks, and yellow flies. No wonder one traveler noted that the shores of the Lower Neuse "seemed almost wholly unsettled, the wilderness appearance being only here and there relieved by the small clearing of a turpentine plantation, fishing establishment, or the twenty-acre field of a 'poor white.' "[5] While prosperous planters such as Nelson journeyed to New Bern to pay their taxes, politick, socialize, buy and sell goods, and—in his case—visit sisters who had married town gentlemen, Garbacon Creek itself remained an isolated backwater community.

The seaport of New Bern, located at the confluence of the Trent and Neuse Rivers approximately thirty miles off the Atlantic, was a center of trade, politics, and society in antebellum North Carolina. By 1850, it was the second largest city in the state with 4,681 residents. New Bern was home to a large, relatively prosperous free black community and was the only place in the state where African Americans accounted for as much as one-fifth of the entire free population.[6] In addition to free blacks, there was also an exceptionally large population of slave laborers who hired out their own time in the city. Slaves who "hired out" contracted their skilled labor for wages and, at the end of the week or month, turned their earnings over to their master. As early as 1794, state legislators exempted New Bern from a law that prohibited masters from allowing their slaves to hire out their time.[7] A shortage of skilled workers necessitated the exemption. Being permitted to exchange their labor for material reward provided slaves with an extra measure of independence—both economic and

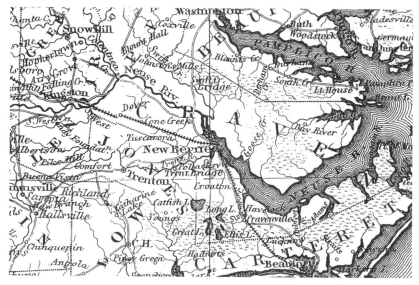

New Bern and vicinity. Detail from "J. H. Colton's Topographical Map of North and South Carolina. A Large Portion of Georgia & Part of Adjoining States." Published in New York in 1861.

psychological—that should not be underestimated. Frederick Douglass underscored the value of this autonomy when he discussed the growing sense of selfhood and desire for freedom that arose from hiring out his time as a ship's caulker in Baltimore: "I became quite restless. I could see no reason why I should, at the end of each week, pour the reward of my toil into the purse of my master. . . . I determined to try to hire my time, with a view of getting money with which to make my escape."[8]

African American strangers were a common sight in New Bern, not at all like Garbacon Creek or the state's other plantation districts. Black sailors and pilots passed through the port regularly and could be seen in the taverns, boardinghouses, and ship's chandleries in the wharf district. Slave fishermen, up from the Lower Neuse, sold their catches at fish markets along the waterfront and hawked oysters and shad through the city streets. Slave watermen and draymen from the state's interior also congregated in New Bern, where they brought their master's cotton bales and turpentine barrels to schooners waiting to carry them to Chesapeake and New England ports. The prominence of free blacks, hired-out slaves, and black maritime laborers all conferred a measure of anonymity to a slave such as Singleton who, as a young boy, ran away to New Bern and concealed himself for three years, working anonymously at the Gaston House Hotel.

By the time he returned to the Nelson plantation, Singleton was old enough to work in the fields. For all of Garbacon Creek's discomforts, its soil was a rich sandy loam ideal for raising the corn, sweet potatoes, beans, and rice cultivated by William Henry Singleton and John H. Nelson's other slaves. According to local legend, the site of the Nelson plantation had originally been a Coree Indian village, and local people still find an abundance of pottery shards and arrowheads there. The land where Singleton toiled had been in the Nelson family since one of Craven County's earliest settlers, also named John Nelson, received a land grant prior to 1706. During the nineteenth century, John H. Nelson and his father, John Sedgwick Nelson, purchased the land surrounding their own from distant relatives.[9]

By the early 1850s, John H. Nelson and his slaves had hewed out a flourishing plantation, and he had become the most prosperous planter in his corner of Craven County. At the beginning of the decade, he owned 26 slaves, among them Singleton's mother, Lettice Nelson, and at least three of her children, William Henry, Hardy, and Joseph Singleton. Nelson's estate, valued at $2,250 in 1850, was 1,000 acres of property that reached south from the manor house at the joining of Garbacon

Creek and the Neuse River. Ten years later, the family patriarch had added 7 slaves and 360 acres to his holdings. Until 1859, John H. Nelson was also the executor of an estate—including 119 slaves—belonging to his wife's young nephew and two nieces. As executor, Nelson was responsible for hiring out these slaves and managing the profits they produced until his young wards reached the age of twenty-one or married. Their comings and goings gave young William Henry Singleton the impression that the Nelson estate was the largest plantation in this secluded corner of Garbacon Creek, which it was, and in all of Craven County, which it was not.

Singleton's master had a unique stature along that cypress-fringed shore of the Lower Neuse. John H. Nelson seemingly took an interest in all aspects of public life. He served on the local school board, as a lay leader in the Adams Creek Methodist Episcopal Church, and took an active interest in Whig politics. Hardly content with the corn shuckings and laying-by festivals that marked plantation life at Garbacon Creek, Nelson and his family also participated in the finer social gatherings in New Bern. Two of his sisters, Ester and Susan, married into the Stanly family, one of the oldest and most prestigious in the county seat. A planter of considerable standing and accustomed to getting his way, John H. Nelson was not the sort of man used to being bested by a slave boy. And yet, each of the three times Nelson attempted to sell the young Singleton, William Henry openly defied his master's authority by running away.

If Nelson was not accustomed to being worn down by a slave's refusal to *stay* sold, he was certainly no stranger to slave resistance and abolitionist sentiments. The late antebellum period is generally described as a time when abolitionist beliefs were least tolerated and least heard in the American South, but in Singleton's *Recollections* not even out-of-the-way Garbacon Creek remained insulated from such revolutionary ideas. Planters such as Nelson had to get used to their bondsmen and women "laying out" as Singleton did, escaping into the surrounding forests or swamps as a temporary protest against especially cruel or unjust treatment. Garbacon Creek was too far from the Neuse's shipping channel for local slaves to have much contact with seagoing vessels, but Singleton and other Nelson slaves often visited New Bern. Along the wharf district, black seafarers spread news of antislavery activity in New England and the West Indies, and a clandestine network of maritime black laborers and white sympathizers had organized a precarious way station of the Underground Railroad. Runaway slaves fled north, first through the local waterways, which were dominated by slave boatmen, and then by sea. Singleton indicates that he knew little of such abolitionist activity, though even he was familiar with "John Brown and the underground railroad" and "a man named Wendell Phillips and a man named Garrison who were getting slaves into Canada." His elders probably knew much more of such matters than he did.

In the years preceding the Civil War, John H. Nelson must have felt besieged by the abolitionism that surfaced even at remote Garbacon Creek. In 1856, his neighbor and cousin, Wiley M. Nelson, freed his thirty-two slaves in his will and provided funds for them to immigrate to Liberia. Wiley Nelson's family unsuccessfully contested the will in court, and the trial marked a major episode in the history of the manumissions movement in North Carolina. The freed slaves sailed in 1858, and the event obviously left a deep impression on the young Singleton. Antislavery politics also erupted in the local church, the site of one of the most memorable episodes in *Recollections of My Slavery Days*. Singleton carefully details the day a visiting white minister invited a slave into the church pulpit, an unusual occurrence in itself, to lead an audience of slaveholders and their slaves in prayer. The slave preacher, Ennis Delamar, dared to recite what Nelson considered an incendiary passage from the Old Testament, and in the midst of a "dinner on the grounds," Singleton's master whipped Delamar and expelled the white minister from the church. It is no wonder that Nelson was a little touchy when it came to abolitionist sentiments, especially since he had to reckon with them inside of his own home. According to Singleton, Nelson's first wife, Eliza, expressed her antislavery beliefs from her deathbed shortly before she passed away. One doubts that she could have entirely concealed her traitorous convictions from her husband.

If antislavery politics and runaway slaves trickled through Garbacon Creek during the antebellum period, they positively deluged the cloistered settlement from the earliest days of the Civil War. Federal forces captured much of the North Carolina coast in late 1861 and early 1862. Union troops held this thin strip of coastline for the remainder of the war, most importantly controlling the seaports of New Bern and Beaufort and all the inlets through the Outer Banks. In his *Recollections*, Singleton celebrates the day in March 1862 when Union troops, under the command of Brigadier General Ambrose E. Burnside, captured New Bern, and he and many others were able to escape to Union lines. At least ten thousand slaves fled to New Bern from parts of eastern North Carolina still in Confederate control. Once inside Federal lines, Singleton and the other fugitives from slavery provided information about Rebel outposts and acted as scouts, guides, and spies for the Union army.

By his own account, Singleton took an active role in pressing the federal government to accept African Americans into the military. Major General John Gray Foster, who assumed command in New Bern after Burnside's departure in July 1862, informed Secretary of War Edwin M. Stanton that he had "received a petition signed by about 120 negroes for arms and organization into the U.S. service." Foster also conceded that he had already armed the same number of former slaves to fortify his lines in a recent attack. The freedmen did not see action, however, and Foster, while noting that they "did their duty well," downplayed their willingness to fight as "self-preservation."[10] Undeterred when told that blacks could not serve in the army, Singleton established his own drilling squad in preparation for the day when African Americans would have the right to fight for their own freedom. That day came in May 1863, when Singleton and a thousand other black men enlisted in the First North Carolina Colored Volunteers, later redesignated the Thirty-fifth U.S.C.T. This was a momentous occasion in the African American freedom struggle, and Singleton's personal memories offer readers a rare firsthand narrative of the events as they unfold. Indeed, throughout *Recollections of My Slavery Days*, one hears the thoughtful, plainspoken voice of a former slave recounting one of the most important chapters in American history. His is only one voice, a single brief vignette, but it speaks to a far broader experience.

* * *

When Singleton wrote *Recollections* in 1922, he was seventy-nine years old. One would not be surprised if he did not recall every detail of his early life in the South, as most of the events that he relates had occurred more than a half century earlier. He had witnessed many of them through the eyes of a slave child whose master had intentionally withheld much knowledge, including literacy. Nevertheless, the vast majority of names, places, and other specific references in *Recollections* can be confirmed in the documentary record. Singleton's story is also highly consistent with the broader narrative of the antebellum era, including the national schism in the Methodist Church over slavery, the outbreak of the Civil War, and the recruitment of African American soldiers. Wiley Nelson truly did manumit his slaves, Federal troops did occupy New Bern from 1862 to 1865, Col. James Beecher was the commanding officer of the Thirty-fifth U.S.C.T., and so on. Not surprisingly, Singleton does get a proper name or two slightly wrong, and he does misspell a few place names. The editors have left his text exactly as it was first published in 1922, correcting these errors in the annotations.

There are also a couple of minor instances in which Singleton's narrative is in conflict with the documentary record. He says, for example, that a "Mr. Ayers" was the presiding elder who invited Ennis Delamar into the pulpit of John H. Nelson's church, but Methodist records indicate that no person by this name served either as a presiding elder or a regular minister in the Methodist Church in antebellum North Carolina. Of course this does not mean that Singleton erred. He may have intentionally concealed the minister's true name. Or, quite possibly, given his relative youth and his relationship to the incident, he might have misunderstood who the minister with the egalitarian streak was. Such inconsistencies are discussed in the annotations.

The most intriguing discrepancy between Singleton's narrative and the documentary record is also one of the most confounding. In *Recollections*, Singleton claims that his master was not John H. Nelson, but John Singleton. Reviewing census records, deeds, and other local documents, we, the editors, found no evidence of a John Singleton residing in Craven County at any time prior to the Civil War. Only after considerable research did we conclude that Nelson was Singleton's real master. Actually, even as Singleton withholds his master's true identity, he leaves a solid trail of evidence in his narrative that leads to Nelson. To begin, in a saga of land transfers and a master's name that cannot possibly all add up, Singleton indicates that his master had acquired his plantation by a marriage to a "Mrs. Nelson, a widow." That was not quite true: the plantation at Garbacon Creek had been in the Nelson family since 1706. At the same time, John H. Nelson's sister, Ester, was a widow until Singleton was about three years old. Given Singleton's perspective as a child, it is easy to understand how he might have confused the exact relations in the Nelson household. But his mentioning the Nelson surname did turn our attention to the Nelson family in Craven County.

Significantly, Singleton's geographical memories map a route that leads directly to Garbacon Creek. He indicates that a "Colonel Nelson" owned the plantation adjacent to his master's plantation; deeds and land grants confirm that Col. Wiley M. Nelson did live next door to his cousin John H. Nelson. Singleton also alludes to the "old Winthrop place" as being in close proximity to his master's land. The Winthrop plantation was one of the oldest in the area, located at the mouth of Adams Creek. As early as 1815, Wiley M. Nelson acquired a tract of the Winthrop land, and in 1855, John H. Nelson also purchased twelve acres from his neighbor John Winthrop. Singleton mentions that when he returned to his mother after being sold to Atlanta, he crossed Adams Creek heading east and walked the few miles home. Adams Creek is a brackish bay, a tributary of the Neuse River, and is located just west of Garbacon Creek. Moreover, the locations of the church and the schoolhouse as delineated by Singleton in *Recollections* fit no other locale than the South River/Adams Creek vicinity where John H. Nelson lived.

Other evidence points not just toward the Nelson plantation at Garbacon Creek, but also directly to John H. Nelson and his family. Singleton says that he had a white father, and his military records and surviving photographs confirm that he was very light-skinned. Census records show that of the twenty-six slaves Nelson owned in 1850, only one was mulatto, an eight-year-old boy; William Henry Singleton would have been close to the same age that year. When describing an incident in which he was whipped for allegedly opening a book, Singleton notes that his master's son Edward, whose books he had been carrying, was "just about my age." John H. Nelson's second son, Edward H. Nelson, was born in 1842, one year before William Henry. Singleton recalls his first mistress's last words well, and acknowledging that he could not remember the exact date of her death, he estimates that it was close to 1858. John H. Nelson's first wife, Eliza Hall Nelson, died on January 28, 1860. Two months later, Nelson married his second wife, Mehetible "Hettie" Mason of Adams Creek, and she became the second mistress of whom Singleton speaks. Additionally, Samuel Hyman, a local boy that Singleton accompanied to the Civil War, was John H. Nelson's nephew. Such convincing familial and geographical evidence removes all doubt that Singleton's master was indeed John H. Nelson.

Knowing that the young William Henry was a slave on the Nelson plantation provides insight into Singleton's own family as well. Surviving records of the Nelson family indicate that Singleton's maternal relatives all belonged to John H. Nelson's father, John S. Nelson. Upon the elder Nelson's death in 1833, his slave property was divided into five lots from which each of his children drew their share of their father's estate. Judging by a predivision inventory of slaves by household and age, Singleton's family included his mother, Lettice, who was then twelve years old; her parents, Jacob and Comfort; and her siblings, Betty, Dick, Nicolas, and the infant Pleasant.[11] The 1833 division of slaves seems to have separated Lettice's family. John H. Nelson drew the lot that included Lettice; Susan T. Nelson received Betty and her infant daughter; while Ester E. Nelson drew the lot which kept Jacob, Comfort, and two of their children, Nicolas and Pleasant, together. Singleton specifically states that he was born in New Bern, not on the plantation, and knowing where each of his family members lived may explain why. Ester Nelson, a widow who eventually married Alexander H. Stanly, resided in New Bern at the time of Singleton's birth. Lettice may have desired the presence of her mother, Comfort, at the birth and so may have journeyed to Ester's home in town. The greater availability of midwives and physicians in New Bern could have been a factor in John H. Nelson's allowing her to go. A healthy child was in both the slave's and the master's best interest.

The only remaining enigma is the identity of Singleton's father, whose name he does not reveal. Like many other firsthand accounts of former slaves, *Recollections of My Slavery Days* points to the heart of the uncertainty of paternity in the slaveholding South. Singleton states that his father was his master's brother and that his being his master's nephew caused the Nelson family great embarrassment. According to Singleton, this was also the primary motivation for John H. Nelson's attempts to sell him away from the plantation. While it is apparently true that Singleton's father was white, he could not have been Nelson's brother. John H. Nelson's only brother, Benjamin F. Nelson, died in 1833, almost ten years too early to have fathered William Henry. Singleton credits his aunt for revealing to him that he was his master's nephew, and the young boy may have misunderstood which white relative or other white man she meant. The aunt herself may have been confused.

William Henry Singleton evidently believed that his father was in fact a Singleton. Slave children of mixed-race heritage commonly retained their white father's surnames; consider the

List of the Names of Negro Slaves —
Belonging to the Estate of John S. Nelson d⚹
and not disposed of by will, — with their age & Value

Names	Age	Valued
Jacob	55	250
Comfort (and Infant child Pleasant)	35	300
Bill	25	425
Betty	16	300
Caroline Infant to Betty	7/12	75
Dick	14	325
Lettice	12	275
Nicholas	6	175
Sealy	60	-100
Daniel	32	425
London — (Infirm)	28	10.0

A part of the inventory of slaves owned by John S. Nelson at his death in 1833. The list includes Singleton's mother, Lettice; his grandparents, Jacob and Comfort; and his aunts and uncles, Betty, Dick, Nicolas, and Pleasant. Estate of John S. Nelson, 1833, Craven County Estate Records, Division of Archives and History.

Lot Nº 1	$	Lot Nº 2	
Jacob	250	Bill	425
Comfort & child	300	Lillie	275
Nicholas	175	Daniel	425
Cain	400	Frank	325
Jim	325	Little Ginny	200
Mary	275	Tom	225
Jack	150	Old Ginny	125
Vilet	300	Edney	300
	2225	Kate	75
To receive in Cash	45		$2375
	$2270	to pay in Cash	105
Drawn by Esther E Nelson		John H Nelson $2270	

Lot Nº 3		Lot Nº 4	
Joe	450	Robbin	475
Ann	250	Aaron	250

Apportionment of John S. Nelson's slaves to his son John H. and his daughter Ester. Nelson bequeathed his slaves to all of his children. The executor of his will divided the slaves among Mary, Benjamin, Susan, Ester, and John H. without regard to keeping the slave families together. Estate of John S. Nelson, 1833, Craven County Estate Records, Division of Archives and History.

example of New Bern's most prominent black slaveholder, John C. Stanly, who was born a slave and whose first and last names were the same as his white father.[12] According to Craven County records, there are only two Singletons who could conceivably have been William Henry's father: Thomas S. Singleton and his son William G. Singleton. Thomas, who in 1850 was a fifty-three-year-old farmer, had property in New Bern, but resided on a plantation in the countryside and owned seventeen slaves. That same year William, a twenty-seven-year-old clerk who never married and apparently owned no slaves, lived at the Washington Hotel in New Bern. If either of these men fathered the slave child, then it would appear that Lettice Nelson had an ongoing affair with him and that the couple had as many as three sons. Singleton's brothers, Hardy and Joseph, shared the surname and remained in the area after the Civil War. In her slave narrative, *Incidents in the Life of a Slave Girl*, Harriet Jacobs of Chowan County, North Carolina, confessed to a similar liaison with a white lawyer who lived near her grandmother. By her own account, she took a lover to foil her master's advances. "[T]o be an object of interest to a man who is not married, and who is not her master, is agreeable to the pride and feelings of a slave." Jacobs wrote, "It seems less degrading to give one's self, than to submit to compulsion." She continued, "There is something akin to freedom in having a lover who has no control over you, except that which he gains by kindness and attachment."[13] Lettice Nelson might have recognized a similar "freedom" in her own situation, if she did indeed have an affair with one of the Singletons. A relationship could have been facilitated if she traveled often between the Nelson plantation and New Bern to visit her mother or other family members owned by John H. Nelson's sisters.

Born in 1797, Thomas Singleton was twenty-four years older than Lettice Nelson, who was born about 1821. An attachment to an older man with money and power might have been attractive to the young slave woman, as it would have conferred prestige and afforded her an extra degree of protection. Given the name evidence, however, it is more reasonable to suggest that Lettice Nelson's lover was William G. Singleton, born about 1823, and that she named her second son after him. Perhaps circumstances prevented the young slave from openly claiming his father's full name, for it appears William Henry Singleton went by the name "Henry" until he moved out of North Carolina after the Civil War Since Singleton's brother Hardy was two years older, and his brother Joseph was two years younger, an affair between Lettice and William G. Singleton would have lasted at least five years.

Did Lettice Nelson reveal the identity of his father to her son William Henry? Or did another family member comment to the young slave one day that the white man across the street was his father? Did Singleton retain this vague memory in the back of his mind even as he began to tell his life story? Perhaps the act of assembling his life into a cohesive narrative had a profound impact on Singleton and forced him to confront, once again, one of the most painful questions he carried throughout his life. Seven years after the publication of *Recollections of My Slavery Days*, when he married his third wife at the age of eighty-seven, it seems that Singleton acknowledged publicly what he might have suspected all along. On the marriage license, he listed his father's name as William Singleton.[14]

* * *

Considering *Recollections of My Slavery Days* in its relation to the African American autobiographical tradition sheds further light upon William Henry Singleton's life and how he chose to live it. Reaching as far back as 1760, born of the struggle to reclaim an autonomous self from the grip of slavery, African American autobiographical texts have operated as an assertion of black identity. The early slave narratives became the means by which the former slaves defined freedom for themselves. Testifying to their life experiences, they also claimed the authority to address the prevailing moral climate of the day.[15] The genre has remained central to black literary production primarily because African Americans have employed it to address racial injustice and challenge white assumptions of the black American experience. As a slave narrative published fifty-nine years after Emancipation, Singleton's text occupies a unique position on this continuum. While *Recollections* contains elements of both antebellum and postbellum slave narratives, Singleton also uses it to address the historical moment from which it emerged.

Literary scholar Stephen Butterfield once observed that "resistance is the backbone of selfhood in African American autobiography."[16] This is certainly true of *Recollections of My Slavery Days*, for in the text Singleton emphasizes his determined will as his most defining characteristic. He relied on it to resist slavery by running away from his masters four times as a child and as a young man. He describes how, on one of these occasions, he traversed nearly six hundred miles posing as the slave of a white woman traveling by stagecoach from Atlanta to Wilmington. He then walked the remaining fifty miles home to Garbacon Creek. This may well be the most extraordinary episode in the autobiography and one of the most important, for it becomes the foundation of the pattern of defiance and resistance upon which Singleton constructs his narrative identity. Moreover, Singleton's escapes must be read as a victory in the battle of wills between the young slave and John H. Nelson, who was equally determined to sell him off the plantation. Recalling these incidents, Singleton repeatedly stresses his own agency in securing freedom for himself.

At the same time, *Recollections* appeared in the post-World War I era, when a resurgence in racial violence extinguished the hope that black participation in the war effort would lead to significant political and social gains. Singleton could not have been oblivious to this reality or immune from its inherent danger. Nor was he the type of man who would have ignored it. Thus, how Singleton tells the story of his life, his language and rhetoric, is as much a part of his ongoing resistance to oppression as the dramatic events of the past he describes.

In many ways *Recollections of My Slavery Days* is similar to antebellum slave narratives, which, as part of the abolitionist arsenal, developed into a stylized rhetorical form. These firsthand accounts provided the most persuasive antislavery argument precisely because they were the personal testimonies of former slaves witnessing to their life experiences. Still, audience expectation shaped these narratives and contributed to the evolution of representative episodes that would have been familiar to most readers. Such episodes might include: tales of slave life on the plantation; references to slave patrols; accounts of the separation of families; reminders that slaves had no rights before the law; and descriptions of the cruelty of masters who whipped their slaves for the slightest infractions.[17] Singleton weaves all of these threads into his story, perhaps because they had been long established as "standards." Additionally, his emphasis on literacy, apparent from the opening paragraphs, was also a crucial component of antebellum slave narratives. As Frederick Douglass's 1845 *Narrative* so clearly reveals, acquiring literacy increased a slave's chance of obtaining freedom, and freedom conferred the power to fashion an identity outside of the prescriptive bounds of slavery.[18] Literacy was also the means by which slave narrators proved indisputably that they were the authors of their own texts and that their testimony was authentic and not wholly the creation of overzealous abolitionists, as some proslavery arguments claimed.

When freedom rendered the antislavery arguments obsolete, African American autobiographers devised new methods for ensuring that their voices would be heard. Postbellum narrators, anxious to aid in the reunification of North and South, focused on black America's contributions to the nation. In the process they often adopted an optimistic narrative stance that reconfigured slavery as a "brief reign of evil" before the dawn of a brighter day.[19] Booker T. Washington's *Up From Slavery* is the best-known example of these changes in the genre. In her 1868 narrative, *Behind the Scenes, or Thirty Years a Slave and Four Years in the White House,* Elizabeth Keckley claims, "Notwithstanding all the wrongs that slavery heaped upon me, I can bless it for one thing—youth's important lesson of self-reliance."[20] Postbellum narrators, like Keckley and Washington, wanted to convince their audience that the former slaves were capable of handling the responsibilities of citizenship.

Recollections of My Slavery Days conforms to this postbellum pattern as well. Singleton grounds the theme of his concluding remarks by quoting 2 Corinthians 5:17: "Ah, we can truly say, 'Old things are passed away; behold all things are become new.' " He then attempts to articulate the gratitude he felt toward the American government for bestowing freedom upon him and his people. This is followed by his prescription for citizenship, "As long as we are honest and obey the law, seek to educate ourselves and to show ourselves worthy of freedom, we will have the respect of the American people and fair treatment from them." Finally, Singleton draws comfort from the fact that African Americans understood "something of the debt" that they owed the nation and showed "their appreciation by trying to be good citizens." And yet the reader detects in Singleton's words a residual, almost ingenuous inability to reconcile the presence of a profound evil with his more hopeful vision of the human condition. How, exactly, is the reader to reconcile the fact that Singleton devotes the majority of the narrative to emphasizing the slaves' agency, especially his own, in securing freedom for themselves with this notion of indebtedness? Singleton's final musings cannot be read outside of the context of his earlier narrative stance nor the historical moment in which he tells his life story. From these perspectives, there lingers an impulse quite different from the cloak of humble gratitude.

Like many African American narrators before him, Singleton faced a potentially hostile audience. Whereas white autobiographers could assume a readership that would grant them the status of "peer," black narrators well into the twentieth century spoke to a predominantly white audience that fundamentally questioned their humanity. The former slaves had to prove that they were brothers and sisters in the human family and that they were faithful transcribers of their own experience. Still, in the antebellum period particularly, black "selfhood" had to be negotiated in an atmosphere in which "truthfulness" and self-preservation were almost mutually exclusive.[21] In much the same way that many slaves adopted a mask of compliance, hiding their interior lives from their masters as a means of resistance and survival, slave narrators concealed certain truths from their audience. The silences of their texts with regard to the details of their escapes speak loudly to this ironic endeavor. Such silences were essential to preserving the clandestine networks through which others might follow them to freedom.

Due to the passage of time, Singleton did not need to omit the details of his days as a fugitive. He even alludes to the slaves' hidden communication network when he confirms that they knew of the abolitionist activities of Brown, Garrison, and

Phillips. Perhaps the most telling silence of *Recollections* is Singleton's apparent failure to comment directly on the racial climate of the days just prior to its publication. In the aftermath of World War I, the Ku Klux Klan had reemerged as a powerful force using violence and intimidation to curtail African American expectations of citizenship. The Klan of the 1920s was a broad-based, middle-class movement of an estimated five million Americans—far more members than during Reconstruction—and at least as popular in the Midwest as in the South.[22] Singleton could not have escaped its influence or the white supremacist ideology that sustained it. Indeed, fear for the safety of family members who remained in the South in the early 1920s could have been one reason Singleton was reluctant to name either his master or his father. Just three years before Singleton published his narrative, in what James Weldon Johnson had characterized as the "Red Summer," race riots broke out in every region of the nation. The tensions that erupted and spilled into the streets in 1919 ranged from competition in jobs and housing, resulting from African American migration northward, to the reluctance of black veterans to return to the prewar status quo and thereby relinquish their ongoing demand for equal treatment under the law.

Singleton was not an activist in the post-World War I era, but he was a veteran, and herein lies the key to understanding what dwells just beneath the surface of *Recollections of My Slavery Days* and its apparently contradictory narrative postures. Foremost, the rhetorical strategy Singleton employs throughout his auto-biography operates from an assumption that had been a crucial aspect of the black freedom struggle since the Revolutionary War: as a soldier, he had earned the right of citizenship. When a Connecticut officer refuses to provide him with arms for self-defense and insists that blacks will never be given the chance to fight in the Civil War, Singleton replies, "The war will not be over before I have had the chance to spill my blood." In the opening paragraphs, he asserts, "I wore the uniform of those men in Blue, who through four years of suffering wiped away with their blood the stain of slavery and purged the Republic of its sin." Like the postbellum narrators who preceded him, Singleton stakes a claim for African American participation in the political and social life of the nation. The value that he places on military service may show a tragically flawed sense of manhood, but it was one deeply rooted in the American experience and exactly the one that white America was most likely to understand. And, like the activists of his day, Singleton consciously draws a parallel between his own wartime experience and those of African American soldiers in World War I. He declares, "[W]hen a nation across the seas sought to enslave the world as once my race was enslaved, I saw the boys of my race take their place in the armies of the Republic and help save freedom for the world."

Singleton's avowal of equality is underscored by his calling attention to the fact that he votes: "Now I feel that I am a part of the country, that I have an interest in its welfare and a responsibility to it." With pride, he describes going to the polls on election day and emphasizes that his vote counts as much as any other man's, regardless of their differing stations in life.[23] Perhaps too optimistically, Singleton celebrates the fact that millions of other African American men shared the same privilege; he fails to mention that few black men in the South had the right to vote in 1922. Nevertheless, Singleton's inclusion of these potentially "subversive" assertions of the rights of citizenship indicates that there is a powerful message behind the mask he assumes in order to avoid alienating his white neighbors in Peekskill and his larger white audience. Without a doubt, contemporary African American readers would have recognized these partially concealed political gestures in the same way that their forebears had understood the hidden messages of freedom in slave spirituals.

* * *

Singleton says little about his life after slavery in *Recollections,* but again, he provides no shortage of clues to aid us in following him throughout his later years. After being mustered out of the Union army in Charleston, South Carolina, in June 1866, Singleton stayed in that city long enough to procure a primer in a local secondhand bookstore and immediately set out to master the alphabet, a task he began as a soldier.[24] Due to the threat of white retaliation for his military service, Singleton felt that he could not return to Craven County and so moved north to New Haven, Connecticut, where he married his first wife, Maria Wanton, in 1868. Journeying to New Haven, Singleton followed a path well worn by African Americans from his birthplace; early migration from North Carolina to New Haven retraced coastal trade routes. Well before the Civil War, at least one group of New Bern's black artisans had settled in New Haven, and their success compelled other free blacks and fugitive slaves to follow. Another primary factor in Singleton's decision to settle in New Haven may have been the connection between that city's African Methodist Episcopal Zion (A.M.E.) church and the A.M.E. Zion church in New Bern, where Singleton drilled his men for the war effort. Andrew's Chapel, later renamed Saint Peter's, had been home to New Bern's black Methodists since 1838. When, in 1862, the A.M.E. Zion's New England Conference sought to establish a mission in the rebelling states, its members targeted Andrew's Chapel as a most likely site. Bishop James W. Hood, who had served as the pastor in New Haven's A.M.E. Zion church from

1856 to 1859, was the missionary who arrived in New Bern in 1864 and successfully persuaded the members of Andrew's Chapel to align themselves with his denomination.[25]

Shortly after arriving in New Haven, William Henry Singleton took an active role in Hood's former church, serving as a trustee and Sunday School superintendent. According to Richard A. G. Foster, who later wrote a brief chronicle of that city's oldest A.M.E. Zion congregation, Singleton may well have been the "most outstanding member" in the church's history.[26] Settling into a quiet life, Singleton worked as a coachman for the prominent Trowbridge family, and in 1884, Maria gave birth to their only daughter, Lulu W. Singleton. As he tells us in *Recollections*, Singleton increasingly felt the call to preach. He began leading evening services at his church, and following Maria's death in 1898, he embarked on a new career as an itinerant minister and moved to Portland, Maine. While there, he married his second wife, Charlotte Hinman. After a brief stint in New York City, the Singletons relocated to Peekskill in 1907, where the aging veteran worked as a gardener and caretaker. A local historian once noted that Singleton was well known for his eloquence and was called upon frequently to address audiences on "patriotic occasions."[27]

Two years after the publication of *Recollections of My Slavery Days*, the Singletons moved back to New York City. Following Charlotte's death in 1926, Singleton returned to New Haven, probably to be close to his daughter, Lulu, and his grandchildren. He married his third wife, Mary K. Powell, in 1929. Despite his declining health, Singleton continued to take part in local patriotic celebrations as a member of the Connecticut G.A.R. The day after he died in Des Moines, the *New Haven Evening Register* celebrated Singleton's life in a front-page article. They preserved the title "Colonel," bestowed upon him by the black soldiers

Singleton had once drilled in New Bern in 1863.[28] His funeral was held on March 13, 1938, at Varick Memorial A.M.E. Zion Church, the same church Singleton had joined upon first arriving in New Haven. African American Masons carried Singleton to his grave where the Connecticut National Guard fired three volleys as a bugler played taps.[29]

William Henry Singleton's final resting-place is in a plot reserved for Civil War soldiers at New Haven's Evergreen Cemetery. The graves surround a large monument commemorating the battles and the service rendered the nation by Connecticut men during the war. Singleton lies closest to the monument on the side where "New Berne" is engraved. His simple stone marker reads "Henry Singleton" and, as is customary for all soldiers, is equal in size and appearance to the rest. One presumes, given the personal significance of New Bern to him, as well as his lifelong pride as a veteran, that this is just the way Singleton would have wanted it.

Recollections of My Slavery Days

by

William Henry Singleton

I

I have lived through the greatest epoch in history, having been born August 10, 1835, at Newbern, North Carolina.[1] That was not so many years, you see, after the adoption of the Declaration of Independence and the winning of the Revolutionary War. But in the country of the Declaration of Independence, I was born a slave, for I was a black man. And because I was black it was believed I had no soul. I had no rights that anybody was bound to respect. For in the eyes of the law I was but a thing. I was bought and sold. I was whipped. Once I was whipped simply because it was thought I had opened a book.

But I lived to see the institution of slavery into which I was born and of which I was for many years a victim pass away. I wore the uniform of those men in Blue, who through four years of suffering wiped away with their blood the stain of slavery and purged the Republic of its sin. I met, too, that great man who led those men as their great Commander-in-Chief; he shook hands with me, yes, talked to me. I can still see his sad, tired worn face as he spoke to me that day. And in those days since I was whipped simply because it was thought I had opened a book, I have seen the books of the world opened to my race. And with the help and sympathy of God's good people I have seen them make a beginning in education. And in my old age when a nation across the seas sought to enslave the world as once my race was enslaved, I saw the boys of my race take their place in the armies of the Republic and help save freedom for the world.

Comparing my position now, living in a good home, with my wife, with friends, respected in my community, with the same rights that every other man has, those days of my boyhood seem like a dream. But folks who know my story like to hear me tell about those days, how we lived, what we thought about, how we were treated, what kind of people our masters were. So I recall them for my friends and for other folks, who, though they do not know me, might like to hear a true story that may seem as strange to them, however, as a fairy tale.

Now although I was born black and a slave, I was not all black. My mother was a colored woman but my father was the brother of my master.[2] I did not learn this until some years later. It caused me much trouble. They were a high proud family, the Singletons.[3] My master's estate was one of the largest in Craven county, North Carolina, and he had more slaves than any other planter thereabouts.[4] The first thing I remember is playing on the plantation with my little brothers and the other slave children. While the men and women slaves were in the cotton, corn, and potato fields working during the day, we children were taken care of by an old slave lady at a central house.[5] She had grown too old to work and so acted as a kind of nurse for the slave children during the day.[6] I was about four years old at the time. I had two brothers younger than I and one two years older.[7] Nights we went home with our mother. The slaves lived in a row of houses a ways from the main house where our master lived. Of course my mother was supplied with all the food we wanted and we did not need much clothing because the weather was warm. I had nobody that I called a father. I only knew my mother. Her name was Lettis Singleton.[8] All the slaves on the plantation had the same name as their master. The slaves on the Singleton's plantation, for instance, were known as Singleton's men and women. John Winthrop had a plantation adjoining ours and all the slaves on that plantation were called Winthrop's slaves.[9] When a plantation changed owners the slaves changed their names. Our plantation had been formerly owned by Mrs. Nelson, a widow. The slaves were then known as Nelson's slaves. When Singleton married Mrs. Nelson, he succeeded to the plantation and all of the slaves, including my mother, were called from that time on Singleton.[10]

I remember my mother used to tell us about our great grandmother. She, like my grandmother, was the slave of a family living in the city of Newbern.[11] I cannot remember the name of this family now. My great grandmother had a hand that was burned and I can remember my mother telling us about it. It evidently made a great impression upon me, for that is about the only thing I can remember from my first years on the plantation, that and the days we spent together at the central house in charge of the old nurse while our mother was away with the other slaves at work in the fields.

One day when I was about four years old a strange man came to this central house where all of us children were and asked me if I liked candy. I told him yes. So he gave me a striped stick of candy. Then he asked me if I liked him. I said, yes, sir, because he had given me the candy. There was a colored woman with him and he asked me then how I would like to go and live with him. Of course I did not know him nor the woman, but without saying any more the man took me away with him and gave me to the strange woman who took me to Atlanta, Georgia, and delivered me to a white woman who had bought me. That night when my mother came to get me and my brothers I was not there. I had been sold off the plantation away from my mother and my brothers with as little formality as they would have sold a calf or a mule. Such breaking up of families and parting of children was quite common in slavery days and was one of the things that caused much bitterness among the slaves and much suffering, because the slaves were as fond of their children as the white folks. But nothing could be done about it, for the law said we were only things and so we had no more rights under the law than animals. I believe it was the more cruel masters, however, who thus separated families.[12] I learned afterwards that the reason I was sold was because there had been trouble between my master and his brother over me and as my presence on the plantation was continually reminding them of something they wanted to forget my master sold me to get me out of the way. I suppose they sold me cheap for this reason. I was bought by a white woman in Atlanta, a widow, who ran a slave farm. That is, she would buy up young slaves whose pedigrees were good and would keep them til they grew up and sell them for a good price. Perhaps she would have taught them to do something and thus add to their value. These slave farms were quite common.[13] Most of the work of the South in those days was done by slaves. Slaves were ginners, that is, they knew how to run cotton gins; they were carpenters, blacksmiths, ship carpenters and farmers. An ordinary slave sold for from $500 to $600 to $700, but a slave of good stock who was a good carpenter or a good ginner would be worth from $1,000 to $1,500.[14] And when such a slave got on a plantation he would not be apt to be sold. They would keep him on the plantation to do their work. So it was to a slave's advantage to learn to do some work, because then he would be treated better and would not be sold. A slave like that would have his wife and he would be of higher standing among the other slaves. But his children, of course, would belong to his master and he would have no legal right to keep his wife if his master chose to take her away from him. But a slave that was lazy or shiftless or inclined to run away would not be wanted on a plantation and he would be sold for almost nothing.

Young as I was when I was sold for the first time I did not like the idea of leaving my mother and brothers. And I did not like my new mistress, either. Not that she treated me so very bad. I was too young to work much so I stayed around the house. I had all I wanted to eat. Of course I had hardly any clothes, but then I did not need many clothes to keep me warm. I did not have any bed to sleep on, simply slept on the dirt floor by the fireplace in the house like a little dog. But my mistress had a great habit of whipping me. Some slave owners used to have a custom of whipping their slaves frequently to keep them afraid. They thought it made them more obedient. My mistress had a bundle of twigs from a black walnut tree with which she used to whip me. My particular work was in running errands and in carrying things from one place to another, and if I did not come back from doing what she told me to do as soon as she thought I should, she would whip me. One day when I was about seven years old, she sent me on an errand. I must have been gone entirely too long for when I returned she started for the whip to whip me again. I suddenly decided to run away, and I did. After I had started I was afraid to come back. My mistress's farm was a little ways outside of Atlanta and I ran into the city. There on the streets I ran across an old colored man who asked me my name and what part of the country I was from and what my mother's name was. When I had told him, he said: "I know your people. I was sold from that part of the country." Then he told me about my great grandmother and her burned hand and how she lived at Newbern. He pointed out the road that led to Newbern and said I might get a ride on the stage. "But don't tell anybody your name," he said, "if they ask you your name, you don't know, and keep agoing." Not long afterward, I saw a stage standing up before a building. So I waited around to see when it would start. Finally I saw a white lady with a carpet bag coming toward the stage and I went and took her carpet bag and helped her in the stage. The colored man who drove the stage thought I belonged to the white lady, because of that fact. It proved that the lady was going by stage route from Atlanta to Wilmington, North Carolina.[15] Of course the same horses and driver that started from Atlanta did not make the whole journey to Wilmington. The horses were changed and the first driver went back, and a new man took the stage until the next change was made. But as all the drivers thought I was with the white lady and as she seemed to be willing to help me by letting them think so, I got to Wilmington in that manner. There the white lady said to me, "Little boy, I have got to stop here and I do not go any further." She did not want me to go with her any further. I suppose she knew I was running away and sympathized with me, but she did not want to get in any difficulty herself, for she did not ask me my name and cautioned me that I did not know anything about her.[16]

From Wilmington I walked and caught rides the rest of the distance to Newbern. It was a city I should judge about as large as Peekskill is now, perhaps a little larger.[17] I remembered what the old colored man in Atlanta had told me to do when I reached there, ask for an old colored woman with a burned hand. My great grandmother must have been quite a well known character in the city, for soon I was directed to where she lived. When I knocked at the door the old colored woman who came to the door wanted to know what I wanted. I told her I was looking for my great grandmother. She asked me who I was. I was afraid to tell her and so said, "I don't know." She said, "You little fool, how is anybody going to know what you want? Are you the little runaway boy that the white people were here looking for?" I said, "I don't know." While we were talking there we heard some men coming. My great grandmother said, "You better get away." Her house was next to the jail.[18] She was owned by a man named Jacobs at that time. I afterwards learned that he was a great friend of the colored people.[19] So I ran and hid myself back of the jail until the men were gone. Then I started from Newbern down the road to the plantation where my mother was. I walked in the road, but if I heard any one coming I would go in the woods and wait until they passed. As it happened, nobody molested me and I made the journey from Newbern to the plantation in about a day and a night. In order to reach the plantation I had to cross a creek, Adams Creek.[20] When I reached there a little before dusk, I saw a man fishing a little ways from the shore. I knew he must be a colored man, because the white people as a rule did not fish, they generally got their fish without taking the trouble.[21] So I hailed the man and asked him if he could put me across the creek. He said he could and pulled to shore and I got in. When he saw how young I was he said, "Look here, little boy, where are you going?" I said, "I don't know." He said, "How am I going to tell where to put you?" I said, "Put me over across the creek? This is Adams Creek?" He said, "Yes." "I want to go to the Singleton plantation. Do you know where that is?" He said, "Oh, yes." He was a colored man, as I had supposed. I said, "My mother's name is Lettis." He said, "Oh yes, I know Aunt Let, I know her well, you go right straight down the road until you get to the schoolhouse and when you get there keep to your left hand. The road will take you right into the Singleton plantation."[22] So he put me ashore on the other side of the creek and I followed his directions and in a little while I came to the school house and then after that it was not long before I was running down the road that led to the plantation and home. It was the only home I knew. It was where my mother was.

37

II

Luckily, the first door I knocked at when I reached the Singleton plantation happened to be the door of my mother's house, but of course I did not know my mother, so when she opened the door and asked me what I wanted, I made my usual reply, "I don't know." I did not know my mother and she did not know me. She said, "What do you want, little boy?" I said, "I am looking for my mother." "Your mother?" "Yes, ma'am." Just then my older brother, Hardy, came to the door and said, "Mamma, that's Henry." My mother said, "No, it isn't; that child wouldn't know how to get back here alone like that. When he went from here he was nothing but a baby." But Hardy said, "Mamma, that's Henry, that's our Henry." Hardy was two years older than I and so was about nine years old then. He was big enough to be working on the plantation. My mother said, "I won't believe it's Henry except I can see a scar on the back of his neck where he was burned; I burned him when I was smoking my pipe one night and when he went away that scar was plain on the back of his neck. If it's there now, I will believe it's Henry." But when I heard her say that I was afraid because I did not know that I had a scar there and I thought it was a trap to catch me and turn me over to the white people. So I ran, but Hardy ran me down and caught me and mother found the scar and then I was all right. We went in the house and I was telling them about my trip when we heard the patrol coming. The patrols were something like our mounted police, they were men who rode around the country and if they found any colored people off the plantations where they belonged, they would lash them and turn them over to their masters. Nights they would go around to the houses where the slaves lived and go in the houses to see if there was anybody there who had no right to be there. If they found any slave in a house where they had no right to be, or where they did not have a permit to be, they would ask the reasons why and likely arrest them and whip them.[23] My mother had a board floor to her house and underneath that a cellar. It was not exactly a cellar, but a hole dug to keep potatoes and things out of the way. When she heard the patrol coming she raised up one of the boards of the floor and I jumped down in the cellar and when the men on the patrol came in they did not find me. That cellar was my hiding place and sleeping place for three years. My mother fed me and looked out for me, and although the white people suspected me and looked for me they could not find me. They got me finally, however, by a trick. One Sunday morning my mother and brothers went to a camp meeting and left me in the cellar. There were cracks in the cellar through which I could see out of doors. Looking out I saw there were some biscuits on a fence not far away. That was one of the tricks the masters had to catch slaves who were in hiding. They would put food on the fences where a slave they suspected of being in hiding could see it in the hope that he would get hungry and venture out and take it and thus reveal himself. This is what happened to me, for no sooner did I go out after the biscuits than I heard a horn blow and soon I was surrounded and caught. They sold me that time to the overseer on the plantation, John Peed. But he did not buy me to keep me on the plantation, he bought me to send me to Jones County, North Carolina, to his folks.[24] He paid $500 for me. But when he sent me to my mother's house to get my clothes to take with me I ran to the woods. They tried to find me, but they could not. Nights I came back to my mother's house and to the cellar and very early in the morning before the sun was up I would go to the woods and watch the men go to their work. I would stay in the woods all day and then come back at night. Of course I could not have done this if the colored people had not been friendly to me.[25] Finally my mother got notice that if

I would come back and give myself up they would put me to work on the plantation, helping the boys feed the horses and things of that kind, that Mr. Peed did not own me anymore for they had given him his money back when I ran away. So I gave myself up, but very soon the folks up at the big house began to find fault about my being on the place, so my master sold me the third time. He virtually gave me away, for he received only $50 for me and sold me to a poor white woman of the neighborhood. She was very good to me. She had a little farm and was what might be called one of the "poor whites." The plantation owners considered anyone who did not own a good deal of property and slaves poor. She was named Mrs. Wheeler.[26] But she got tired of me for some reason and sold me to a party who was to come for me. But before they could come to take me away I ran away. I went to the city of Newbern and hired out as a bell boy at the Moore Hotel. Of course they did not know that I was a runaway slave and they did not know my name, either, for I would not tell them. They called me the "Don't know" boy. But they gave me three dollars a week and my food.[27] I was then about ten years old. I stayed at the Moore House three years. I left because some of the other colored boys about there had found out who I was and said they were going to give me away. So I went back to the plantation again to my mother's house. She told me that they had promised not to sell me any more if I would give myself up and go on the plantation and go to work. And she wanted me to do that, because she was very tired of my foolishness, as she called it, running away and going about the country. So I did give myself up. I went to the big house and saw my master and told him I had come home to stay now. He was a tall, raw-boned, black-faced man, quite old then, too old to go to war when the war came.[28] He said, "All right, go out to the barn and go to work and it will be all right. Go out and help the men take care of the horses and stay home." And I did. I learned to plow and to do all kinds of work about the plantation and in the cotton and corn fields. I was not given any chance to learn a trade, though. And of course I was given no opportunity to learn to read. There was no school for the slaves to attend. I would not have wanted to go to school any way for my only experience with a book was not a pleasant one. One day my master's son, who was just about my age, had a bag coming home from school and he gave me the bag to carry.[29] The bag had books in it. I slung the bag over my shoulder but did not take any of the books out. But Edward said I took one of his books out of the bag and opened it. When his father heard that, he said he would teach me better things to do than that, and he whipped me very severely. I cried and told him that I did not take the book out, and then he whipped me all the harder for disputing his word. He whipped me with a harness strap. That was not the first time my master whipped me, however. Whipping with him was a very common thing. He was one of the masters who believed in whipping their slaves to keep them in subjection. If you looked cross at them, they would whip you. They did not see the propriety of treating their slaves well to get more work out of them.[30]

It was shortly after this that I learned my master was not only my master but my uncle and that his brother was my father.[31] I learned this from my aunt.[32] She heard about my master whipping me and she said, "It is a great note for him to whip you for that, because you are his own nephew." That surprised me very much. I had heard the men about the plantation before speak about my being half white, but I did not know why. My aunt also told me that once my master and his brother had had a quarrel about it up at the big house. But by that time I had settled down on the place and so there was no more said about it. Except once my master's daughter, who very much resembled her mother for her good disposition, referring to the fact said there oughtn't to be so much trouble about it anyway because we were one family and the time would come when the black people would be free.[33] This made her father very angry. She had heard those things, I think, from her mother. It was her mother who had owned the plantation originally, as I have before mentioned. Upon her husband's death she later married John Singleton, and he then became master of the plantation.[34] But I think they never agreed upon the question of having slaves. She did not like the idea of owning slaves. She was a good Christian woman and she believed the Bible did not teach that it was right to own slaves. Shortly before her death an incident occurred which made a very great impression upon all of us for more reasons than one. She was very sick and one day she called Frank, the carpenter, and who as the head slave had charge of all the others, and told him to bring into her room all the slaves he could find on the plantation.[35] They were shelling corn at the time, getting it ready to ship to market, and he brought in as many as he could get together, I suppose, in a short time. I was not one of them, but I was later told by the others what happened. She said to them, "Be good and do your work and the time will come when you will all be free. The North is not satisfied with slavery." My master's brother was present and heard this and after that we were treated much worse than before. Whenever they saw a group of us standing together they would come up and make us disperse for fear we were going to raise against them. Shortly after that our mistress died and on the day of the funeral all of us slaves on the plantation, between seventy-five and a hundred, men, women, and children, followed her body to the cemetery, about five miles away, where she was buried.[36]

It was a very sad occasion, for all the women were crying and most of the men too, as well as the children. We knew that she was the best friend we had and that now our lot would be harder.

Shortly after that my master married again, but our new mistress did not have the kind heart that our old mistress had had.[37]

I do not remember just the year our mistress died and told us that we would some time be free, but I think it was about 1858. At any rate, it was not long before we began to hear talk of a war. Our masters were afraid that there would be a war. They kept talking against the North. They told us that white people in the North were nothing but shop slaves. That the white girls were slaves who did house work for the Northern people and that the Northern people were not considered as high class as the Southern people.[38] It was about this time, too, that we first heard of a man named Lincoln. They said he was a bad man and that he had horns. Another man we heard about was John Brown and the underground railroad.[39] Of course we did not understand what the underground railroad was. We thought it was some sort of road under the ground. We only knew, of course, what we were told. We could not read or write and if any of us had tried to learn to read or write we would have been severely punished. One reason for the prejudice which the plantation owners had against the poor white people in every community was that these poor white people naturally sympathized with us and the plantation owners were afraid that because of this they might teach us to read or might give us some information about what the North was trying to do.[40] So we learned little about the outside world. We did learn, however, that a man named Wendell Phillips and a man named Garrison were getting slaves into Canada and we were told that once you got into Canada they could not get you back again, that you were free.[41] Of course the slaves as a whole wanted to be free. Many of them were not treated well and the thought of being sold was a very burdensome thing. The slaves on our plantation had been told that they were going to be free, and they were looking for what their mistress had said to come true. Then

Colonel Nelson, who owned an adjoining plantation, set all his slaves free by his will when he died and they were all sent to Liberia. There were about seventy-five of them.[42] And we were anxious to be free too.

I do not mean by all this that our life was altogether bad. We had enough to eat and we had certain pleasures. It was a common thing for the slaves to have parties where the slaves from adjoining plantations came together and danced and sang and played. The masters encouraged these parties for the purpose of getting the young men and women slaves acquainted with one another. They were looked forward to with pleasure, for they were the chief social events. Another thing we liked to do was attend the camp meetings.[43] We liked the singing and the speaking. And then it was something for us to go to. One of the worst features of slavery was that the slaves on a plantation were virtually in prison. They could not leave the plantation except with the consent of their masters. Then no matter how hard they worked they had nothing which they could call their own. Even their children did not belong to them. And they themselves were liable to be sold away to a distant part of the country to a master whom they did not know and who might be very cruel to them. Then as there were no schools for us and as we could not read you can see how we would want to go to camp meetings or to church. So we were always glad when Sunday came. On Sunday, masters and slaves all went to church together.

Our master was a very religious man, being a local preacher in the Methodist church.[44] Once every three months the Presiding Elder used to visit the church and hold a quarterly meeting after he preached.[45] On one of those visits an incident occurred that I still remember after so many years. It showed how bitter our masters were toward any one who sympathized with us. And it marked, too, the breaking off of religious association between our part of the South and the North.[46]

III

I cannot remember when the church incident with relation to the Presiding Elder occurred, but it could not have been so very long before the beginning of the war. We slaves used to go to the same church our master and the other plantation owners attended. Of course we used to sit back by the door by ourselves while they sat up front. The church was about five miles away from our plantation.[47] We slaves used to walk while our masters rode. This Sunday for some reason they left me at home. But after they were gone I happened to think of a donkey I often rode and the thought occurred to me that I might ride him to church. So I got on his back and started off. He carried me to church in good style but when we reached there instead of waiting for me to get off he threw me off. I had no rope to tie him, so I left him outside and went in the church. The result was that he got in a fight with another donkey while the church service was in progress and created such a disturbance that I was later given a severe whipping for it.

But another thing happened during that service which caused a greater commotion than my donkey. Mr. Ayers, the Presiding Elder, called upon a colored man named Ennis Delamar to pray. Ennis was a slave who had recently been purchased by my master and who had quite a local reputation as a religious man.[48] The fact that Mr. Ayers should call upon a slave to pray caused great offense to the plantation owners and after the service was over and while the masters and their families were arranging themselves on the ground to eat their dinner, my master called Ennis to him and asked him what he meant by asking God to send the time when Ethiopia should stretch forth her arm like an army with banners, and said he would teach him better than to use words such as that.[49] Of course Ennis could not make any reply to this. He had simply been repeating what he heard some white men say, because he himself could neither read nor write. However, they gave him a severe whipping right then and there. This seemed to disturb Mr. Ayers very much. He withdrew from the company and went over to where the slaves were preparing their dinner and told them that he did not see why a Christian man could not be allowed to use his gift of prayer even if he was black. In some way this remark got back to the white people. So when the afternoon meeting was called my master told Mr. Ayers that his service was no longer wanted and that he need not visit the church any more. From that time on my master had charge of the meetings as local preacher and we never saw Mr. Ayers again.[50]

This incident, as I say, must have happened a short time before the beginning of the war, because shortly afterwards, Samuel Hymans, a young man from our community who was attending West Point, came home from vacation, but when the vacation was over he did not return to West Point. Instead he commenced to organize a company of soldiers. I was very anxious to go with him as his servant and my master, at his request, let me do so.[51] The reason why I was anxious to go with Hymans was because I wanted to learn how to drill. I did learn to drill. After Fort Sumpter was fired upon, Hyman's company went to form with other companies at Newbern, the First North Carolina Calvary.[52] This regiment was stationed at Newbern until the 14th of March 1862, when Burnside and Foster captured Newbern and drove our regiment to Kinston.[53] At Kinston, I ran away from the regiment and made my way to Burnside's headquarters at

Newbern.[54] I secured employment as the servant of Col. Leggett, of the 10th Connecticut Regiment.[55]

I told the Colonel my story, but I found out later that my story was not believed and that they thought I had been sent by the rebels to secure information for them about the Union troops. I soon had an opportunity, however, to convince them of my honesty. A stranger was brought into the camp and brought to headquarters as a suspicious person. He would give no information about himself and no one, of course, knew anything about him. Finally I was sent for and asked if I knew the man. I replied that I did, that he was Major Richardson of the First North Carolina Calvary.[56] After giving this information I was sent out of the room and later the adjutant on General Foster's staff came to me and told me I must not be too positive about this man because he was a Union man. My reply was, "If I am not correct, you can cut my throat." He told the guard to keep a watch over me, that they had not got through with me. So I was held until they could secure further information. They secured the information the next day that I was a slave and had been a servant for one of the officers in the First North Carolina Calvary and that it was a fact that I had run away from there. This information was securred [*sic*] from Colonel Leggett, for it was by his sentries that I was picked up when I came into the Union lines. Then I was taken to General Burnside's headquarters and asked the best way to reach the rebels at Wives Forks, before you could get into Kinston.[57] I laid the route out for them the best I knew how, but said that if I were going to command the expedition I would give them a flank movement by way of the Trent River, which was five miles farther from Wives Forks than the Neuse River. But they did not accept my proposition and attacked directly, with a result that they were repulsed.[58]

I took part in that attack as a guide and had a horse shot from under me.[59] A few days later I told Colonel Leggett that I would not fight any more unless I was prepared to defend myself. He said, "We never will take niggers in the army to fight. The war will be over before your people ever get in." I replied, "The war will not be over before I have had the chance to spill my blood. If that is your feeling toward me, pay me what you owe me and I will take it and go." He owed me five dollars and he paid me. I took that five dollars and hired the A.M.E. Zion Church at Newbern and commenced to recruit a regiment of colored men.[60] I secured the thousand men and they appointed me as their colonel and I drilled them with cornstalks for guns.[61] We had no way, of course, of getting guns and equipment. We drilled once a week. I supported myself by whatever I could get to do and my men did likewise.

I spoke to General Burnside about getting my regiment into the federal service but he said he could do nothing about it. It was to General Burnside, however, and my later association with him, when I was with him for a time as his servant, that I owe what I now regard as one of the greatest experiences of my life. It was one day at the General's headquarters. His adjutant pointed to a man who was talking to the general in an inner room and said, "Do you know that man in there?" I said, "No." He said, "That is our President, Mr. Lincoln." In a few minutes the conference in the inner room apparently ended and Mr. Lincoln and General Burnside came out. I do not know whether they had told President Lincoln about me before or not, but the General pointed to me and said, "This is the little fellow who got up a colored regiment." President Lincoln shook hands with me and said, "It is a good thing. What do you want?" I said, "I have a thousand men. We want to help fight to free our race. We want to know if you will take us in the service?" He said, "You have got good pluck. But I can't take you now because you are contraband of war and not American citizens yet. But hold onto your society and there may be a chance for you." So saying he passed on. The only recollection I have of him is that of a tall, dark complexioned raw boned man, with a pleasant face. I looked at him as he passed on in company with General Burnside and I never saw him again.[62]

On January 1, 1863, he signed the Emancipation Proclamation, which made me and all the rest of my race free. We could not be bought and sold any more or whipped or made to work without pay. We were not to be treated as things without souls any more, but as human beings. Of course I do not remember that I thought it all out in this way when I learned what President Lincoln had done. I am sure I did not. And the men in my regiment did not. I had gone back to Newbern then. The thing we expected was that we would be taken into federal service at once. It was not until May 28, 1863, however, that the thing we hoped for so long came to pass, when Colonel James C. Beecher, a brother of Henry Ward Beecher, that great champion of our race, came and took command of the regiment.[63] I was appointed Sergeant of Company G, being the first colored man to be accepted into the federal service and the only colored man that furnished the government a thousand men in the Civil War.[64] The regiment was at first called the First North Carolina Colored Regiment. It later became known as the 35th Regiment, United States Colored Troops. Soon afterwards we were armed and equipped and shipped to South Carolina and stationed at Charleston Harbor. From that time until June, 1866, when we were mustered out at Charleston, South Carolina, I was in active service, ranking as First Sergeant, 35th U.S. Colored Infantry. J. C. White was the Captain of that company and Colonel James C. Beecher was the commander of the regiment.[65] We saw active service in South Carolina, Florida, and Georgia.[66] I was wounded in the right leg at the battle of Alusta, Florida.[67] After the war ended we were stationed for a time in South Carolina, doing guard duty and were finally mustered out of the service on June 1, 1866. My honorable discharge from the service dated on that day, although it is worn and not very legible now, as you can see, is one of my most prized possessions. Some years ago a man from the government service in Washington made out for me in a detailed form a record of my war service. It is in much more complete form than I have set it down here, but I think such details are of more interest to one's family than to the general public.

My life since the war has been the ordinary life of the average man of my race. I have not so many accomplishments to boast of, but I have done the best I could to prove myself worthy of being a free man. I came North shortly after the war and settled in New Haven, Connecticut.[68] I secured a position as a coachman with a very estimable family, the Trowbridges. I worked six years for Henry Trowbridge and then after his wife died I went to work for his brother, Thomas R. Trowbridge, for whom I worked for twenty-five years.[69]

Shortly after the war ended I was converted in a Methodist church, of the A.M.E. Zion connection, in North Carolina, so when I came to New Haven I joined the A.M.E. church in that city.[70] It was in that church that I learned to read, although I had learned the alphabet and how to spell simple words while I was in the army.[71] I became ambitious to learn all I could and so read as many books as I could and availed myself of all the opportunities that presented themselves to educate myself. I saved some money from my salary, too. After the war my mother and brothers remained near Newbern and hired a little place known as the Salter place.[72] When I had money enough I bought this place. But there was such a strong feeling against me at Newbern for the part

I had taken in the war, that I could not go back there. The Ku Klux Klan said they would shoot me. My mother lived on the place until her death some years later. But I could not even go back to see her buried. My brothers remained on the place long after that, but they did not live very long after my mother. Then I sold the place through a Mr. Wheeler of Newbern. I sold it for $300 more than I gave.[73]

As a result of my study and interest in religious things I gradually began to speak in the church in New Haven. Finally I was ordained a deacon and later I was ordained a local elder. I conducted for some years the religious services at the jail in New Haven and took part in the city mission work as an assistant to the preacher in charge of that work.[74] After my thirty-one years of service with the Trowbridges, I entered the itinerant minstry, devoting all my time to it for three years as a preacher in the A.M.E. Zion church in Portland, Maine.[75]

It was in New Haven, too, that I married my wife. She was a Northern girl, Maria Wanton.[76] Our married life was very happy. We had one daughter. She is married and lives in New Haven. Her husband's name is Charles Fitch. She is the mother of eight children, two of whom died in infancy. The other six are all active, healthy boys.[77] My wife died in 1898. Later I married my present wife. She was Charlotte Hinman; also a Northern girl, a resident of Staten Island. She has made me a good wife and we have been very happy.[78]

At the end of my three years as pastor of the church in Portland, I resigned from the itinerant work and came to New York City, where I worked until about 1906, when I came to Peekskill, New York which has since been my home.[79] I worked first at the LeBaron place on Main Street. Later I was employed by Mr. George F. Clark, on Crompond Street, for whom I worked for thirteen years.[80] During the World War I was for a time engaged in work with the local Y.M.C.A. and the War Camp Community Service. Since the war I have been employed by Mr. George W. Buchanan of Peekskill.[81] I have been extremely fortunate in my employers. From all I have received kind and considerate treatment, vastly different from the rough, sometimes brutal treatment I received from my slave masters. It is as different, in fact, as freedom from slavery. It is impossible, I think, for those who have always been free to realize the difference. Now I feel that I am a part of the country, that I have an interest in its welfare and a responsibility to it. As a slave I was only property, something belonging to somebody else. I had nothing to call my own. Now I am treated as a man. I am a part of society. I am a member of the Admiral Foote Post G.A.R., of New Haven, Connecticut, which I joined in 1879. I was for a year chaplain of the Post, resigning when I went to Portland. I am also a member of the Oriental Lodge, F. and A.M., of New Haven, Connecticut.[82] Since coming to Peekskill I transferred my church membership to the Mt. Olivet Baptist Church of Peekskill.[83] And I am a citizen of this great country and have a part in directing its affairs. When election day comes I go to the polls and vote, and my vote counts as much as the vote of the richest and best educated man in the land. Think of it! I, who was once bought and sold, and whipped simply because it was thought I had opened a book. And it is not only I who have this privilege, but millions of other men of my race. Ah, we can truly say, "Old things are passed away; behold all things are become new."[84]

I feel that I am greatly indebted to the government and to the American people for what they have done for me and for my race. I can not find words to express properly what I feel. But my heart is overflowing with gratitude, when I think of my situation and the situation of the people of my race now, and think of all the blessings we enjoy, compared with our former situation. I feel that as long as I live an honest life, do my work and conduct myself properly, I have the respect and the good wishes of the community. And this is true, I believe, not only of myself but of every man of my race. As long as we are honest and obey the law, seek to educate ourselves and to show ourselves worthy of freedom, we will have the respect of the American people and fair treatment from them.

It is a great thing to have lived to see this day come. It is great to feel that the people of my race understand something of the debt they owe this great country and are showing their appreciation by trying to be good citizens.

God has been very good to me. I have preached His gospel. I can read His book. America has been very good to me. I am one of its citizens. There is no stain on the Flag now. I once fought under its banner. The Great Emancipator is loved by the world now. He once shook hands with me.

Truly I can say with the psalmist, "The lines are fallen unto me in pleasant places; yea, I have a goodly heritage."[85]

William Henry Singleton at a 1937 Grand Army of the Republic reunion in Gettysburg, Pennsylvania. Photograph courtesy of Laurel Vlock, New Haven, Connecticut.

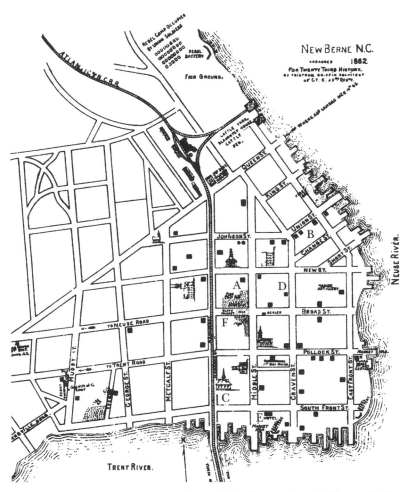

Map of New Bern, North Carolina, 1862. Key: A-Stanly House; B-Slover House; C-Andrew's Chapel, Methodist Episcopal Church; D-Jail; E-Gaston House Hotel; F-Slave Market. Map, with minor changes, from James A. Emmerton, *A Record of the Twenty-third Regiment, Mass. Vol. Infantry, in the War of the Rebellion, 1861-1865* (Boston: William Ware, 1886), facing p. 92.

The Gaston House Hotel on South Front Street, New Bern. William Henry Singleton lived and worked at this hotel, owned and operated by William P. Moore, for nearly three years during one of his escapes. Photograph from the William Garrison Reed Collection, New Bern-Craven County Public Library.

African American volunteers for the Union army in front of the Broad
Street Episcopal Church, New Bern, ca. 1863. Illustration from *Frank
Leslie's Illustrated Newspaper*, February 27, 1864.

General Ambrose E. Burnside. Under his command, Union troops captured New Bern in March 1862. They held the town and much of the North Carolina coast for the remainder of the war. When Burnside left New Bern in July 1862, William Henry Singleton accompanied him as a manservant. It was apparently during this time that he met Abraham Lincoln. Copy of photograph from the files of the Division of Archives and History.

The Charles Slover House, one of Burnside's headquarters, located on the southwest corner of Johnson (Union) and East Front Streets, New Bern. Photograph from the files of the Division of Archives and History.

The John Wright Stanly House, on the southwest corner of New and Middle Streets, served as another headquarters for Burnside. Photograph from the files of the Division of Archives and History.

Major General John G. Foster, appointed by Burnside as military governor of New Bern. In 1864, Foster assumed command of the Department of the South. Portrait from *The National Cyclopædia of American Biography*, vol. 10 (New York: James T. White, 1900), 134.

Colonel James C. Beecher, brother of renowned abolitionists Henry Ward Beecher and Harriet Beecher Stowe, commanded the Thirty-fifth United States Colored Troops, in which William Henry Singleton served. Portrait from *The National Cyclopædia of American Biography*, vol. 3 (New York: James T. White, 1893), 131.

Troops of Colonel Edward A. Wild's African Brigade liberating slaves in North Carolina. In May 1863, Wild arrived in New Bern to begin organizing black troops. Those African American men who had already been drilling, like Singleton, were among the first recruits. Illustration from *Harper's Weekly*, January 23, 1864.

The Battle of Olustee, Florida, February 20, 1864. William Henry Singleton fought in this battle. Two officers and twenty men from the Thirty-fifth United States Colored Troops died that day, and 131 men were wounded. Illustration from *Harper's New Monthly Magazine*, 33 (November 1866): 718.

H.M.SNYDER.

Bishop J. W. Hood of the African Methodist Episcopal Zion Church. Hood arrived in New Bern in 1864 to establish a Zion congregation at Andrew's Chapel. He remained in North Carolina and played an active role in Reconstruction politics. William Henry Singleton joined Hood's former church when he migrated to New Haven after the war. Portrait from J. W. Hood, *The Negro in the Christian Pulpit* (Raleigh: Edwards, Broughton, 1884), frontispiece.

William Henry and Maria Singleton's only daughter, Lulu Singleton Fitch. Born in New Haven in 1884, Lulu married Collins Fitch in 1905. The couple had seven sons and one daughter. Photograph courtesy of Leroy Fitch, New Haven, Connecticut.

William Henry Singleton was laid to rest in the Civil War veterans' plot of New Haven's Evergreen Cemetery. His first wife, Maria, and daughter, Lulu, are buried several hundred yards away. Photograph by Roderick Topping, New Haven, Connecticut.

Appendix A

Chronology

August 10, 1843: William Henry Singleton is born in New Bern, North Carolina. His mother, Lettice Nelson, is a slave on the John H. Nelson plantation at Garbacon Creek in Craven County. His father, most likely William G. Singleton, is a white man who resides in New Bern. Growing up, Singleton will be known as "Henry."

May 1-June 11, 1844: The Ninth General Conference of the Methodist Episcopal Church convenes in New York City. On June 6, southern conferences announce their plans to form a separate organization known as the Methodist Episcopal Church, South. The church would not be reunified until 1939, one year after William Henry Singleton's death.

Ca. 1848: John H. Nelson sells the five-year-old Henry to a slave trader, who takes the young Singleton to a plantation near Atlanta.

Ca. 1851: After approximately three years, Singleton runs away from Atlanta. Posing as the slave of a white woman traveling alone, he arrives in Wilmington, North Carolina, walks the remainder of the way to New Bern, crosses Adams Creek in Craven County, and returns to the Nelson plantation.

Ca. 1851-1854: Henry Singleton lives on the Nelson plantation but escapes detection by hiding in the root cellar of his mother's cabin.

Ca. 1854: Luring the young slave out of hiding, John H. Nelson tries to sell him again. Singleton claims Nelson sold him to the overseer of the plantation, but before he is taken away, he escapes to the woods.

1855: John H. Nelson purchases twelve acres of land from his neighbor, John Winthrop. After Nelson's third attempt to sell him, Singleton runs away to New Bern, where he lives and works at the Gaston House Hotel for three years.

1856: Colonel Wiley M. Nelson dies. In his will, he frees his thirty-two slaves and provides them with funds to go to Liberia.

Ca. 1858: Henry Singleton returns to the John H. Nelson plantation at Garbacon Creek.

May 1, 1858: Colonel Wiley M. Nelson's former slaves sail for Liberia.

October 16, 1859: John Brown leads raid on the federal arsenal at Harpers Ferry, Virginia.

1860

Samuel O. Hyman Jr. lives at the New Bern Hotel, operated by John F. Jones.

William G. Singleton resides at his mother Harriet's house and works as a customs collector.

January 28: Eliza Hall Nelson, John H. Nelson's first wife, dies.

March 26: John H. Nelson marries Mehetible (Hettie) N. Mason.

1861

April 12: Confederate troops fire on Fort Sumter, South Carolina.

June 21: Samuel O. Hyman Jr. enlists in Company K, Second Regiment, North Carolina State Troops.

August 23: As a private in Company K, Hyman and his manservant Singleton proceed to Camp Advance, near Garysburg in Northampton County.

September-December: Singleton remains with Hyman, whose company is stationed at Smith's Battery, near Camp Potomac in King George County, Virginia.

1862

March 14: Brigadier General Ambrose E. Burnside's Union troops defeat Confederate general L. O'B. Branch and his men in the Battle of New Bern. Federal troops will occupy New Bern for the remainder of the Civil War.

Late March/Early April: Singleton escapes to Union lines in New Bern from nearby Goldsboro. He first works for Lieutenant Colonel Robert Leggett of Company K, Tenth Connecticut Infantry Regiment.

July 7: Singleton accompanies Burnside from New Bern to Fort Monroe in Virginia.

July 9: Lincoln meets with Burnside at Fort Monroe. Singleton meets the president as Lincoln departs after his conference with Burnside.

Fall/Winter: Singleton returns to New Bern.

1863

January 1: Lincoln signs the Emancipation Proclamation, freeing all the slaves in areas still in a state of rebellion.

May 18: Colonel Edward A. Wild of the Thirty-fifth Massachusetts arrives in New Bern to begin recruiting an African American regiment.

May 27: Twenty-year-old Henry Singleton enlists as a sergeant in Company G, First North Carolina Colored Infantry.

1864

January 24: Bishop J. W. Hood arrives in New Bern to establish the first African Methodist Episcopal Zion mission church in the South.

February 8: The First North Carolina Colored Infantry is redesignated the Thirty-fifth United States Colored Troops (U.S.C.T.) and attached to Montgomery's Brigade in the District of Florida.

February 20: Sergeant Singleton is wounded at the Battle of Olustee, near the Suwannee River, in Florida.

November 25: The Thirty-fifth U.S.C.T. is ordered to Hilton Head, South Carolina.

November 30: Singleton's regiment fights in the Battle of Honey Hill, near Grahamville, South Carolina. Afterward, the troops return to Florida.

March 1865: The Thirty-fifth U.S.C.T. is ordered to Charleston, South Carolina, where they are stationed for the remainder of the war.

June 1, 1866: Sergeant Singleton is mustered out of service in Charleston.

Ca. 1867: William Henry Singleton moves north.

1868: In New Haven, Connecticut, Singleton marries his first wife, twenty-one-year-old Maria Wanton, who was born in Middletown, Connecticut.

1871: Singleton first appears as a resident of New Haven, Connecticut, in the city directory. He is also listed as a trustee at the local A.M.E. Zion church, the oldest African American church in New Haven. This same year he begins working for Henry Trowbridge.

1872: Singleton is the clerk of trustees and the superintendent of Sabbath schools at his church, which moves from its original location on Dixwell Avenue to Foote Street and is renamed the Foote Street A.M.E. Zion Church.

1877: Singleton begins working as a coachman for Thomas R. Trowbridge.

1882: Singleton serves as treasurer of New Haven's Oriental Lodge, No. 15.

October 6, 1883: Civil War veteran Singleton joins the Admiral Foote Post, No. 17, Department of Connecticut, Grand Army of the Republic (G.A.R.).

1884: The Singletons' daughter, Lulu W., is born in New Haven.

1886: Singleton is a local preacher at the Foote Street A.M.E. Zion Church. The Reverend W. H. Abbott is the church's pastor.

1893-1895: Singleton serves as chaplain for the Admiral Foote Post, No. 17, G.A.R.

May 15, 1898: On a Sunday evening, as her husband preaches, Maria Singleton dies in church.

1899-1901: Singleton moves to Portland, Maine, where he is the pastor at the A.M.E. Zion church, located on Mountfort Street. In 1899, he marries Charlotte Hinman, originally of Staten Island, New York.

1902: No longer a pastor, Singleton works as a teamster in Portland.

1903: The Singletons move to New York City. They live there for three years.

1905: Lulu W. Singleton, age twenty-one, marries Collins L. Fitch in New Haven.

1907-1924: The Singletons reside in Peekskill, New York. Shortly after their move, Lillian E. LeBaron hires Singleton as a gardener. By 1915, he is working as a coachman for George F. Clark. Later, the couple lives at the home of George W. Buchanan, where an elderly Singleton works as a caretaker. By July of 1924, the Singletons are living again in New York City.

1915: The modern Ku Klux Klan receives its charter in Fulton County, Georgia.

1917: The United States enters World War I and the 369th Infantry becomes the first black combat unit to serve overseas. Approximately three hundred thousand African Americans serve in the war. Following a race riot in East Saint Louis, W. E. B. Du Bois and James Weldon Johnson lead ten thousand people down New York City's Fifth Avenue in the Negro Silent Protest Parade.

1919: Beginning in June and extending through October, race riots erupt in major cities throughout the United States.

March 18, 1922: The first installment of *Recollections of My Slavery Days* appears in the *Highland Democrat*, a local weekly newspaper in Peekskill. The remaining episodes are published consecutively in the next three editions of the paper. Later in the year, the *Highland Democrat*'s press will publish Singleton's slave narrative as a pamphlet.

1925: In Washington, D.C., forty thousand members of the Ku Klux Klan march down Pennsylvania Avenue.

January 13, 1926: Charlotte Singleton dies at Harlem Hospital in New York. Later in the year, William H. Singleton moves back to New Haven.

September 2, 1929: At the age of eighty-six, Singleton marries his third wife, fifty-three-year-old Mary K. Powell.

1936: Singleton is the oldest member participating in the G.A.R. encampment in Washington, D.C.

1938
July 1-4: Singleton attends the seventy-fifth reunion of Union and Confederate veterans at Gettysburg.

September 7: After walking fifteen blocks in the afternoon parade at the seventy-second reunion of the G.A.R. in Des Moines, Iowa, William Henry Singleton dies at approximately 8:45 P.M. Following his funeral at the Varick Memorial A.M.E. Zion Church a week later, Singleton is buried at Evergreen Cemetery in New Haven.

Appendix B
Genealogy

WILLIAM HENRY SINGLETON FAMILY TREE

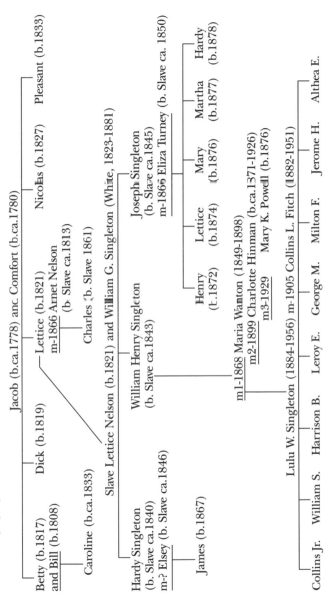

Slaves belonging to John S. Nelson (d.1833)

Jacob (b.ca.1778) anc Comfort (b.ca.1780)

Betty (b.1817) and Bill (b.1808)

Dick (b.1819)

Lettice (b.1821)
m-1866 Arnet Nelson
(b. Slave ca.1813)

Nicolas (b.1827)

Pleasant (b.1833)

Caroline (b.ca.1833)

Charles (b. Slave 1861)

Slave Lettice Nelson (b.1821) and William G. Singleton (White, 1823-1881)

Hardy Singleton
(b. Slave ca.1840)
m-? Elsey (b. Slave ca.1846)

William Henry Singleton
(b. Slave ca.1843)

Joseph Singleton
(b. Slave ca.1845)
m-1866 Eliza Turney (b. Slave ca. 1850)

James (b.1867)

Henry
(t.1872)

Lettice
(b.1874)

Mary
(b.1876)

Martha
(b.1877)

Hardy
(b.1878)

m1-1868 Maria Wanton (1849-1898)
m2-1899 Charlotte Hinman (b.ca.1371-1926)
m3-1929 Mary K. Powell (b.1876)

Lulu W. Singleton (1884-1956) m-1905 Collins L. Fitch (1882-1951)

Collins Jr.

William S.

Harrison B.

Leroy E.

George M.

Milton F.

Jerome H.

Althea E.

John S. Nelson Family of Garbacon Creek, Craven County

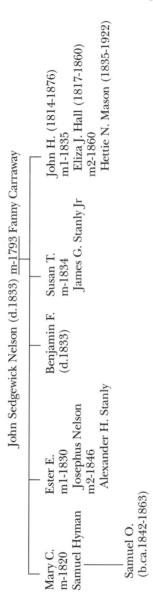

John H. Nelson Family of Garbacon Creek, Craven County

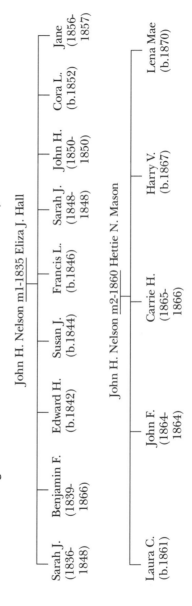

SINGLETON FAMILY OF NEW BERN

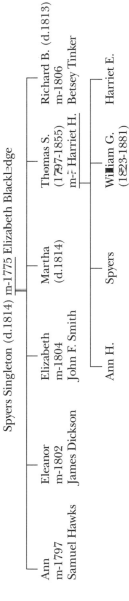

Spyers Singleton (d.1814) m-1775 Elizabeth Blackledge

Ann
m-1797
Samuel Hawks

Eleanor
m-1802
James Dickson

Elizabeth
m-1804
John F. Smith

Ann H.

Martha
(d.1814)

Spyers

Thomas S.
(1797-1855)
m-? Harriet H.

William G.
(1823-1881)

Richard B. (d.1813)
m-1806 Betsey Tinker

Harriet E.

Notes

Introduction

1. *New Haven Evening Register*, September 8, 1938.

2. *Recollections of My Slavery Days* originally appeared in four consecutive issues of the newspaper. *Highland Democrat* (Peekskill, N.Y.), March 11, 25, April 1, 8, 1922.

3. The 1850 population of Craven County included 7,220 whites, 1,538 free blacks, and 5,951 slaves. U.S. Bureau of the Census, *Statistical View of the U.S., Compendium to the Seventh Census* (Washington, D.C.: Government Printing Office, 1854), 278 (hereafter cited as *CSC*).

4. Applying to the Freedman's Savings & Trust Company for a loan in 1874, Henry Payten said he was born on the Neuse River "down in Egypt." Payten had been a soldier in Company A of the Thirty-fifth U.S.C.T., which was Singleton's regiment. North Carolina Freedman's Savings & Trust Company Records, National Archives, Washington, D.C. (microfilm, State Archives, Division of Archives and History, Raleigh; State Archives hereafter cited as NCSA).

5. Thomas Kirwan, *Soldiering in North Carolina* (Boston, 1864), 6.

6. Guion Griffis Johnson, *Ante-Bellum North Carolina: A Social History* (Chapel Hill: University of North Carolina Press, 1937), 114, 583; Alan D. Watson, *A History of New Bern and Craven County* (New Bern, N.C.: Tryon Palace Commission, 1987), 293-307. For exact population figures, see *CSC*, 371.

7. Johnson, *Ante-Bellum North Carolina*, 531-532.

8. Frederick Douglass, *Narrative of the Life of Frederick Douglass, An American Slave, Written By Himself* (New York: Penguin Classics, 1986), 139.

9. For an excellent and thorough discussion of Nelson landholdings and genealogy, see Dollie C. Carraway, *South River: A Local History from*

Turnagain Bay to Adams Creek, 2d ed. (Fayetteville, N.C.: M and L Designs, 1994), chaps. 7-9.

10. *The War of the Rebellion: A Compilation of the Official Records of the Union and Confederate Armies*, ser. 3, 3:192 (hereafter cited as *OR*).

11. Betty also had an infant daughter named Caroline, whose father presumably was the slave Bill, also living in Jacob and Comfort's quarters. Estate of John S. Nelson, 1833, Craven County Estates Records, NCSA.

12. Loren Schweninger, "John Carruthers Stanly and the Anomaly of Black Slaveholding," *North Carolina Historical Review* 67 (April 1990): 161 (journal hereafter cited as *NCHR*).

13. Harriet Jacobs, *Incidents in the Life of A Slave Girl, Written by Herself*, ed. Jean Fagan Yellin (Cambridge, Mass.: Harvard University Press, 1987), 55.

14. William H. Singleton and Mary K. Powell Marriage License, September 2, 1929, Connecticut State Department of Health, Bureau of Vital Statistics, National Archives, Washington, D.C. (National Archives hereafter cited as NA).

15. William L. Andrews, *To Tell A Free Story: The First Century of Afro-American Autobiography, 1760-1865* (Chicago: University of Illinois Press, 1988), xi. This groundbreaking text provides one of the best discussions of the antebellum slave narrative genre as a whole.

16. Stephen Butterfield, *Black Autobiography in America* (Amherst: University of Massachusetts Press, 1974), 18.

17. James Olney delineates these rhetorical standards in "I Was Born: Slave Narratives, Their Status as Autobiography and as Literature," in *The Slave Narrative*, ed. Charles T. Davis and Henry Louis Gates Jr. (New York: Oxford University Press, 1985), 148-175, especially 152-153.

18. Douglass, *Narrative of the Life of Frederick Douglass*, 78-79, 81, 82-87.

19. For an excellent discussion of postbellum slave narratives, see Francis Smith Foster, *Written by Herself: Literary Production by African American Women, 1746-1892* (Bloomington: Indiana University Press, 1993), 117-118, 123-124, 131.

20. Elizabeth Keckley, *Behind the Scenes, or Thirty Years a Slave and Four Years in the White House* (New York: Oxford University Press, 1988), 19-20.

21. Andrews, *To Tell A Free Story*, 3.

22. Nancy MacLean, *Behind the Mask of Chivalry: The Making of the Second Ku Klux Klan* (New York: Oxford University Press, 1994), xi.

23. Leroy E. Fitch confirmed that his grandfather remained loyal to the party of Lincoln and was a staunch Republican throughout his life. Telephone interview with Katherine Mellen Charron, March 1, 1999.

24. *New Haven Evening Register*, September 8, 1938.

25. The full details of African American migration from North Carolina to New Haven is a story waiting to be told. Various sources lay the foundation for preliminary discussion. See James W. Hood, *One Hundred Years of the African Methodist Episcopal Zion Church* (New York: A.M.E. Book Concern, 1895), 290-293; William S. Powell, ed., *Dictionary of North Carolina Biography*, vol. 3 (Chapel Hill: University of North Carolina Press, 1988), 195-196; Robert Austin Warner, *New Haven Negroes: A Social History* (New Haven, Conn.: Yale University Press, 1940), 15, 26, 125, 128-130, 169-170, 192.

26. Richard A. G. Foster, "Short History of Varick Memorial African Methodist Episcopal Zion Church, New Haven, Conn.," *A.M.E. Zion Quarterly Review*, 56 (winter 1946): 17-21.

27. Chester A. Smith, *Peekskill, A Friendly Town: Its Historic Sites and Shrines: A Pictorial History of the City From 1654-1952* (Peekskill, N.Y.: Friendly Town Association, 1952), 166.

28. *New Haven Evening Register*, September 8, 1938.

29. *New Haven Journal-Courier,* September 12, 1938; *New Haven Evening Register,* September 14, 1938.

Recollections of My Slavery Days

1. There is some uncertainty as to the actual year of Singleton's birth. Additional evidence indicates Singleton was born in or around 1843. The personal description of Singleton at the time of his enlistment into the Union army in May 1863, and replicated on his 1898 application for a veteran's pension, reads: "Age 20 years, height 5ft, 6in; complexion light; eyes grey; hair black; born New Berne N.C.; name of owner not found." In later pension applications, Singleton claimed a variety of birth years—1835, 1842, 1843, and 1845—indicating that he probably did not know the exact year he was born but knew that he was close to twenty years old when he enlisted. Later in the narrative, Singleton mentions that he was about the same age as his master's son when the war began. John Handcock Nelson was Singleton's master and his second son, Edward H. Nelson (1842-1877), is listed as nineteen years old in the 1860 census. This lends credence to the validity of Singleton's age in his war records as well. Finally, Singleton also claims that his brother Hardy was two years his senior. Hardy Singleton appears in the 1870 census as a thirty-year-old farmer, meaning that he would have been born around 1840 or 1841. Thus, the date of Singleton's birth is most likely August 10, 1843. His 1938 obituary, however, states that Singleton was 103 years old when he died. Singleton's "Newbern" is New Bern today. For information on Singleton's date of birth, see Henry Singleton, Declaration for Pension, April 9, 1898; February 21, 1907; October 8, 1913; July 28, 1924; January 25, 1929; Mary K. Singleton, Declaration for Widow's Pension, October 15, 1938, War Department, Record and Pension Office, NA. See also Descriptive Books of the Thirty-fifth, Thirty-sixth, and Thirty-seventh Regiments of the United States Colored Troops, NCSA. On Edward H. Nelson and Hardy Singleton, see Eighth and Ninth Censuses of the United States, 1860 and 1870: Craven County, North Carolina, Population Schedule, NA (microfilm, NCSA), census hereafter cited by year, county, and

schedule. One of Singleton's obituaries appeared in the *New Haven Evening Register*, September 8, 1938.

2. Singleton, a mulatto, does seem to have had a white father, but it could not have been his master's only brother, Benjamin F. Nelson. Benjamin died in 1833, almost a decade too early to have fathered William Henry. Will of Benjamin F. Nelson, 1833, Craven County Wills, NCSA.

3. The Singletons had been a prominent family in New Bern around the turn of the nineteenth century. Spyers Singleton, the first of the family in Craven County, married Elizabeth Blackledge in 1775, and the couple had two sons and four daughters. By 1815, Spyers, his son Richard B., and daughter Martha had died, while the three remaining daughters had all married. As of 1834, two of these daughters, Ann Hawks and Elinor Dickson, had relocated to Gadsden County, Florida, and Greene County, Alabama, respectively. Therefore, the only Singletons remaining in Craven County by the time of William Henry Singleton's birth were Thomas S. and his two sons. In 1850, Thomas S. was a fifty-three-year-old farmer who owned seventeen slaves and a house in New Bern but resided in Craven County. His son William G. Singleton, unmarried, lived in New Bern and apparently owned no slaves, while son Spyers resided in nearby Hyde County. Significantly, Thomas's brother had died long before Singleton's birth, and Thomas himself died in 1856 and so cannot be the master of which Singleton speaks. For information on the Singletons, see Craven County Marriage Records, Register of Deeds Office, New Bern (hereafter cited as RDO-NB); Will of Spyers Singleton, 1814, and Will of Martha Singleton, 1815, Craven County Wills, NCSA; Estate of Richard B. Singleton, 1813, Craven County Estates Records, NCSA; Ann Hawks, March 11, 1834, Book 50, p. 236, Craven County Deeds, and Elinor Dickson, 1834, Book 51, p. 26, Craven County Deeds, RDO-NB. For details of Thomas S., William G., and Spyers Singleton, see Will of Thomas S. Singleton, 1856, Craven County Wills, NCSA; 1850 Census: Craven County, N.C., Population and Slave Schedules.

4. This would be the John H. Nelson plantation at Garbacon Creek, on the south side of the Neuse River, in what was then the easternmost part of Craven County, nearly fifty miles from the county seat of New Bern. In 1883, Garbacon Creek become part of Carteret County, whose county seat, Beaufort, lay only twenty miles south. The Nelson plantation totaled one thousand acres and was valued at $2,250 in 1850. At the time, Nelson owned twenty-six slaves, only one of whom was a mulatto, an eight-year-old boy, most likely Singleton. Singleton's claim that John H. Nelson owned more slaves than his neighbors can be explained by the fact that Nelson became the legal guardian of his wife's nephew and two nieces, and subsequently, had charge over all of their slaves in 1848. Eliza Hall Nelson was John H. Nelson's wife. Her brother, Josephus, died in 1843, and when his wife, Julia Ann Hall, died in 1848, the couple's children were left in the care of their aunt and uncle. John J., 11; Eliza J., 10; and Josephine, 5, are listed as members of the Nelson household in the 1850 census. Josephus Hall's will stipulated that his son would receive his share of the estate when he reached the age of twenty-one; his daughters, at the age of eighteen or upon their marriage, whichever came first. While the number of Hall slaves living on the Nelson farm from 1850 to 1858 is indeterminate, the children divided their father's estate—including 119 slaves—among themselves in 1859. Prior to this division, John H. Nelson would have managed all of the Hall children's slaves. By 1860, John J. Hall had moved out of his uncle's household and taken his slaves with him. That same year, John H. Nelson owned 33 slaves, including two mulatto men, one age 16, probably Singleton; Eliza Hall owned 38 slaves, including one hired out to her uncle; and Josephine Hall owned 38 slaves. Eliza and Josephine are listed as living in the Nelson household, and their slaves appear next to their uncle's in the slave schedule. Thus, there were approximately 110 slaves living on the Nelson plantation, which had grown to 1,390 acres. Of the 690 farms in Craven County in 1860, only 8 exceeded 1,000 acres; of the 674 slaveholders, only 17 owned between 30 and 40 slaves, and only 1 slaveholder owned more than 100 slaves.

For information on the Hall children and slaves residing on the Nelson plantation, see Will of Josephus Hall, 1843, Craven County Wills, NCSA; Estate of Josephus Hall in Account with John H. Nelson,

Executor, July 28, 1852, and Division of Slaves, December 31, 1859, Court of Pleas and Quarter Sessions of Craven County, (Josephus Hall, 1852), Craven County Estates Records, NCSA; Carraway, *South River*, chap. 9. For information on changes in the Carteret and Craven county line, see David Leroy Corbitt, *The Formation of North Carolina Counties, 1663-1943* (Raleigh: State Department of Archives and History, 1956), 58-59; Regarding Carteret County and Craven County farm sizes and slaveholders in relation to the Nelson plantation, see 1850 and1860 Censuses: Craven County, N.C., Population, Agriculture and Slave Schedules; U.S. Bureau of the Census, *Agriculture of the U.S. in 1860, Compiled from the Original Returns of the Eighth Census* (Washington, D.C.: Government Printing Office, 1864), 210, 235.

5. John H. Nelson listed 1,250 bushels of Indian corn, 60 bushels of oats, 100 bushels of beans, 25 bushels of Irish potatoes, 400 bushels of sweet potatoes, and 2,000 pounds of rice as part of the value of his farm in 1850. A sixty-year-old woman was the oldest female slave on the plantation at this time. 1850 Census: Craven County, N.C., Agricultural and Slave Schedules.

6. For an informative discussion of the role of older slave women on plantations, see Deborah Gray White, *Ar'n't I a Woman? Female Slaves in the Plantation South* (New York: W. W. Norton and Company, 1985), 114-118.

7. As previously noted, Singleton refers to his older brother, Hardy, by name later in the narrative. In 1870, Hardy Singleton, a farmer, resided with his wife and son in the Second Township in Craven County. In all probability Joseph Singleton, a thirty-five-year-old African American farm laborer who in 1880 resided with his family in the Fifth Township of Craven County, is one of Singleton's younger brothers. Parents often passed on familial names to the next generation and among Joseph's five children were Henry, 8; Lettice, 6; and Hardy, 2. The identity of Singleton's second younger brother remains unknown. 1870 and 1880 Censuses: Craven County, N.C., Population Schedules.

8. When John Sedgwick Nelson died in 1833, his children inherited his forty-three slaves. In the division of his father's slaves with his brother,

Benjamin, and his sisters, Ester, Susan, and Mary C. Hyman, John H. Nelson drew Lot #2, which included the slave girl Lettice, age twelve. Lettice Nelson would have been approximately twenty-two years old when her second son, William Henry, was born. Estate of John S. Nelson, 1833, Craven County Estates Records, NCSA.

9. John H. Nelson purchased twelve and one-third acres between Adams Creek and Garbacon Creek for sixty dollars from John S. Winthrop in 1855. The land bordered that of Wiley M. Nelson, a cousin, whose plantation was adjacent to John H.'s. John H. Nelson, 1855, Book 62, p. 352, Craven County Deeds, RDO-NB. Dollie C. Carraway also denotes Winthrop's as one of the oldest plantations in the Adams Creek area in the nineteenth century. Carraway, *South River*, 27, 44, 98-99.

10. Slave naming was not as clear-cut as Singleton recalls. Most slaves, if they had a surname, did not change names when they changed owners. Singleton acknowledges this practice himself when he later tells of an incident involving a slave named Ennis Delamar, who had been purchased recently by Singleton's master, John H. Nelson. For a discussion of slave naming prior to Emancipation and the names, or "titles," slaves used among themselves, see John W. Blassingame, *The Slave Community: Plantation Life in the Antebellum South* (New York: Oxford University Press, 1979), 181-183; Charles Joyner, *Down By the Riverside: A South Carolina Slave Community* (Urbana: University of Illinois Press, 1984), 217-222. In his attempt to conceal his master's true identity, Singleton seems to have confused the facts regarding the Nelson-Singleton marriage and ownership of the Nelson plantation. According to county marriage records, the only marriage between a Nelson and a Singleton in Craven County prior to the Civil War was that of a James Nelson and Elizabeth Singleton on December 9, 1817. This couple, however, lived on the north side of the Neuse River, not the south side where William Henry grew up, and their circumstances do not fit those described by Singleton in *Recollections*. Without a doubt, the land that Singleton recalls in his narrative belonged to John H. Nelson.

The Nelson plantation at Garbacon Creek had been in the family since the first John Nelson received a land grant prior to 1706. It remained in the family until Harry V. Nelson, son of John H. and his second wife, Hettie, sold it to George W. Best in 1918. Thus Singleton's claim that the plantation had been formerly owned by a widow Nelson cannot be correct. There was, however, a "widow Nelson" in his world. Ester E. Nelson, John H.'s sister, had married her second cousin Josephus, in 1830. They also lived at Smith's Creek and had a house in New Bern. Josephus Nelson died in 1838, and it appears Ester took up residence in New Bern, where she married Alexander H. Stanly in 1846. Singleton was three years old at that time. Regarding the Nelson-Singleton marriage, see Craven County Marriage Bonds, NCSA. See also John S. Nelson, Books 37-39, 42-44, 50, Craven County Deeds, RDO-NB; John H. Nelson, Books 53-54, 62, 64, 70, 74, Craven County Deeds, RDO-NB; Will of Josephus Nelson, 1838, Craven County Wills, NCSA; Ester E. Nelson, January 21, 1840, Book 54, p. 352, Craven County Deeds, RDO-NB. For an excellent and thorough discussion of Nelson landholdings and genealogy, see Carraway, *South River*, 10-11, chap. 7, and especially chap. 8.

11. While the identity of Singleton's great-grandmother remains unknown, in all probability his grandmother was a slave woman named Comfort who belonged to Ester E. Nelson and resided with her mistress in New Bern. Comfort first belonged to John S. Nelson. Upon the division of the slaves in his estate, Ester drew Lot #1, which included Comfort, age 35. Eugene Genovese has noted that "[m]asters and overseers normally listed their slaves by households," and it appears that John S. Nelson's slaves were listed in family groups before being divided into lots. The first family group contained: "Jacob, 55, Comfort (and infant child Pleasant), 35, Bill, 25, Betty, 16, Caroline—infant to Betty, 7 mos., Dick, 14, Lettice, 12, and Nicolas, 6," which indicates that Comfort was also Lettice's mother. Additional evidence from the 1880 Census substantiates this. The Arne[s]t Nelson household located in the Fifth Township of Craven County comprised wife Lettis, 54; mother Comfort, 100; and son Charles, 19. In keeping with the effort of many former slaves to legitimize their marriages after Emancipation, Arne[s]t Nelson certified in 1866 that he and his wife, who registered her name as Lettice Nelson, had cohabited as man and wife for the previous four

years. Presumably, they were both slaves on the Nelson plantation. If Comfort actually was 100 years old in 1880, she was born ca. 1780 and would have been 53 instead of 35 in 1833, when John S. Nelson's will was proven. Obviously, there are errors in some of these numbers. Comfort also appears in an 1846 marriage agreement between Ester E. Nelson and Alexander H. Stanly. It seems Ester's first husband, Josephus, had been a poor businessman. Not only did he mortgage several tracts of land and quite a few slaves repeatedly in the years prior to his death, but Ester's father, John S. Nelson, specifically stipulated in his will that her slave inheritance could neither become subject to Josephus's control nor that of his creditors. In the Nelson-Stanly document, Ester paid Joseph Fulford, a nephew by marriage, one dollar and put her slaves in his trust, but still retained control over them for as long as she lived. Eugene D. Genovese, *Roll, Jordan, Roll: The World the Slaves Made* (New York: Vintage Books, 1976), 452; Estate of John S. Nelson, 1833, Craven County Estates, NCSA. On Arne[s]t and Lettice Nelson, consult Craven County, N.C., Cohabitation Records, 1866 (microfilm), NCSA, 23. Regarding Josephus Nelson's poor business acumen as it might have affected the Nelson-Stanly agreement, see Will of John S. Nelson, 1833, Craven County Wills, NCSA; Josephus Nelson, March 13, 1834, and October 1, 1834, Book 50, pp. 181-183, 352-354, Craven County Deeds, RDO-NB; Ester E. Nelson and Alexander H. Stanley, May 15, 1846, Book 58, p. 9, Craven County Deeds, RDO-NB.

12. Judging from the estate records of John S. Nelson, the Nelson family felt little remorse in separating slave families. Each family "unit" that appeared in John S. Nelson's slave inventory was divided among five lots based not upon familial relations, but upon their relative value. Estate of John S. Nelson, 1833, Craven County Estates, NCSA. Contrary to Singleton's assertion, however, it was hardly the cruelest masters who separated families. Across the slaveholding South in general, most slaveholders understood the importance of familial ties among slaves and incorporated this knowledge into the fabric of their social control. A "troublesome" slave, for example, might be sold in order to preserve order on the plantation. Conversely, masters might expect to keep their slaves in line by continually subjecting them to the threat of sale. At the same time, a slaveholder's "benevolence" usually extended only as far as

his or her pocketbook would allow. More often than not, economic pressures dictated an owner's decision to sell slaves and thus separate loved ones, although slaveholders did so with varying degrees of conscience. To justify their actions, many white masters claimed that slaves, being less than human, felt no pain upon separation from their children. Still others, when forced to generate income, attempted to sell their slaves to friends or relations living nearby so as to keep the familial bond from being totally severed. Regardless, slaves confronted daily the fear of being separated from family members. For a more complete discussion of the separation of slave families and their attempts at reunion, see Leon F. Litwack, *Been In the Storm So Long: The Aftermath of Slavery* (New York: Vintage Books, 1980), 229-239; Brenda E. Stevenson, *Life in Black and White: Family and Community in the Slave South* (New York: Oxford University Press, 1996), 182-183, 223-225. In her discussion on slavery in Loudoun County, Virginia, Stevenson also traces the changing attitudes regarding the sale of slave youths.

13. The buying and selling of slaves for speculative profit, not merely for their labor, was indeed common throughout the antebellum South. According to James Oakes, "Land and slaves became the two great vehicles through which slaveholders realized their ambitions of fortune." In the minds of many slaveholders, raising slaves for profit was directly linked to upward mobility. In terms of the marketplace, this type of "slave farm" represented a speculative business venture, and those who participated viewed themselves as aggressive entrepreneurs. James Oakes, *The Ruling Race: A History of American Slaveholders* (New York: Alfred A. Knopf, 1982), 50, 52-68, 73-74, 170-174, 226-233.

14. Singleton's estimations of the worth of both unskilled and skilled slaves are consistent with what is known about the value of slaves elsewhere in the antebellum South. Ulrich B. Phillips has noted that in 1848 the average price of an unskilled slave in Georgia was $900, while $700 was the going rate in South Carolina. By 1853, these prices had risen to $1,200 and $900, respectively. Ulrich Bonnell Phillips, *The Slave Economy of the Old South: Selected Essays in Economic and Social History*, ed. Eugene D. Genovese (Baton Rouge: Louisiana State University Press, 1968), 142.

15. Wilmington is located on the Cape Fear River, approximately thirty miles upriver from the Atlantic and eighty miles southwest of New Bern. In 1850 it was the only city in the state that had a population greater than five thousand. By 1860, New Bern's population exceeded five thousand, but Wilmington was still the largest city in the state. Johnson, *Ante-Bellum North Carolina*, 114-115.

16. This may well be the most extraordinary episode in Singleton's narrative for a number of reasons. First, the six-hundred-mile distance between Atlanta and New Bern decreased the likelihood of a successful escape for a slave of any age, and Singleton would have been only five or six years old at the time. Second, his meeting an older slave who was acquainted with North Carolina and with actual members of his family points to a rather remarkable, though not impossible, degree of good fortune. The probability of individual white women abetting runaway slaves should not be discounted. Other former slaves, such as Harriet Jacobs, also recalled instances in their narratives when white women aided fugitives. Yet, this particular white woman seems atypical for the additional reason that she was traveling alone. A woman traveling without an escort was a rare sight in the antebellum South. This was especially true for upper- and middle-class women, which this woman appears to have been. Perhaps discouraging unwanted attention was one reason she allowed the young Singleton to pose as her servant. In actuality, there is no way to know this woman's identity or motivation.

Still, the episode—perhaps embellished in the retelling seventy years later—plays a crucial narrative function. Singleton uses it to establish a pattern of defiance and resistance to slavery upon which he constructs his narrative identity. Alluding to his intelligence and initiative, Singleton emphasizes his own agency in securing his freedom.

On aid to fugitives by white women, see Jacobs, *Incidents in the Life of a Slave Girl*, 99-100. On women and travel in the antebellum South, see Catherine Clinton, *The Plantation Mistress: Woman's World in the Old South* (New York: Pantheon Books, 1982), 8-9, 102-103, 175; Stevenson, *Life in Black and White*, 135-136.

17. New Bern had only 4,681 inhabitants in 1850, as compared to Peekskill's 15,868 in 1920. The population of Craven County in 1850,

however, totaled 14,709—7,220 whites, 1,538 free blacks, and 5,951 slaves. *CSC*, 278, 371; U.S. Bureau of the Census, *Fourteenth Census of the U.S.*, vol. 1, *Population Number and Distribution of Inhabitants* (Washington, D.C.: Government Printing Office, 1921), 262.

18. The New Bern jail was located on Craven Street, where the present rear of the 1884 Craven County Courthouse now stands. Charles Slover, a prominent merchant and later, president of the National Bank in New Bern, owned and lived in the house immediately to the north of the jail from 1834 to 1850. Christ Episcopal Church then purchased the property and rented it out during the 1850s. Thirty-seven-year-old lawyer George F. Stevenson bought the house in 1859 after renting it for several years. Edmund H. Grant owned the house to the west of the jail in 1849 but was residing permanently in Wilmington by 1850. Charles Slover, Edmund H. Grant, and George F. Stevenson, New Bern Town Taxables Records, 1834, 1849, 1859. Original volumes in collection of Tryon Palace Historic Sites and Gardens, New Bern, N.C. See also 1850 and 1860 Censuses: Craven and New Hanover Counties, N.C., Population Schedule.

19. Though Singleton's encounter with his great-grandmother would have occurred sometime in 1850 or 1851, the identity of the person who owned the old slave woman with a burned hand remains a mystery. Of the men who lived near the jail, Charles Slover apparently owned no slaves, while in 1850 George Stevenson owned three slaves, the oldest of which was a forty-five-year-old woman. Benjamin Jacobs, originally of Massachusetts, resided in the Second Ward of New Bern. In 1850, he owned one female slave, age twenty. In 1853, Jacobs, William P. Moore, and Alexander Mitchell purchased a turpentine distillery from Amos Wade, which was located on the road from New Bern to Smith's Creek. Since Singleton later lived and worked at Moore's hotel for three years, it is likely he knew Jacobs personally. There is nothing on record to substantiate Singleton's claim that Jacobs was a friend to African Americans, but New Bern was home to an unknown number of clandestine activists, white and black, who helped fugitive slaves to escape by ship to New England and Canada. Jacobs may have been involved in such abolitionist activity. He appears to have left town shortly

after the Civil War. Amos Wade, March 3, 1853, Book 61, p. 198, Craven County Deeds, RDO-NB; 1850 and 1860 Censuses: Craven County, N.C., Population and Slave Schedules. See also David S. Cecelski, "The Shores of Freedom: The Maritime Underground Railroad in North Carolina, 1800-1861," *NCHR* 71 (April 1994): 174-206.

20. Adams Creek rises in central Carteret County and flows north into the Neuse River, approximately thirty miles east of New Bern. In Singleton's day, this would have been in Craven County. William S. Powell, *The North Carolina Gazetteer: A Dictionary of Tar Heel Places* (Chapel Hill: University of North Carolina Press, 1968), 4.

21. For a comprehensive discussion of slave fishermen in the North Carolina tidewaters and of local African American boatmen who aided fugitive slaves, see Cecelski, "Shores of Freedom." During the Civil War, troops of the Fourth Rhode Island also received aid from black fishermen who rowed them across the Newport River from Morehead City to Beaufort. John G. Barrett, *The Civil War in North Carolina* (Chapel Hill: University of North Carolina Press, 1963), 109.

22. John H. Nelson, Singleton's owner, was one of the original superintendents of common schools in Craven County's Thirty-eighth District, which extended from Adams Creek to Garbacon Creek. Craven County Census School Reports and Settlements, 1841-1861, NCSA.

23. With regard to New Bern specifically, Alan D. Watson has noted that the "zeal" and "violence" of the slave patrols often frightened the women of the town. Alan D. Watson, *A History of New Bern and Craven County* (New Bern: Tryon Palace Commission, 1987), 313. For further insight into slave patrols, see Litwack, *Been In the Storm So Long*, 28.

24. Jones County, formed in 1778 from Craven County, borders Craven to the south. According to census records, there were no Peeds residing in Jones County in 1850 or 1860. The nearest Peeds lived in Beaufort County, which borders Craven County to the north. Of these, only Josephus Peed appears to have lived in the area during the years of Singleton's residency. In 1850, Josephus Peed, originally of South Carolina, was a twenty-seven-year-old farmer who owned four slaves. It is

doubtful that he was the overseer on the Nelson plantation since it was customary at this time for overseers to live at the plantation on which they worked. Powell, *North Carolina Gazetter*, 256-257; Johnson, *Ante-Bellum North Carolina*, 492; 1850 and 1860 Censuses: Beaufort, Craven, and Jones Counties, N.C., Population and Slave Schedules.

25. Fugitive slaves did indeed rely on other slaves for supplies and protection. On the prevalence of this in eastern North Carolina particularly, see Cecelski, "Shores of Freedom," especially 180.

26. When the 1850 and 1860 censuses were taken, no Wheelers were reported residing in or remotely near Craven County. Singleton may have misremembered the family's name, or the Wheelers may not have resided in Craven County for very long, a distinct possibility in an age when many poorer whites were migrating out of North Carolina to take advantage of more fertile, less expensive western lands. 1850 and 1860 Censuses: N.C. Population Schedule; David S. Cecelski, "Oldest Living Confederate Chaplain Tells All? Or James B. Avirett and the Rise and Fall of the Richlands," *Southern Cultures* 3 (winter 1977) especially 18-22.

27. The Gaston House Hotel, known for its "lavish entertainment," was located on South Front Street in New Bern. The local firm of Hughes and Dudley owned and operated the hotel, which was worth seven thousand dollars in 1849, making it one of the most valuable properties in New Bern at that time. William P. Moore appears to have purchased and assumed operations of the hotel in the early 1850s. A longtime resident of the town, Moore seems to have been a well-known local businessman who had built his fortune as the turpentine industry swept through New Bern in the 1840s. By 1849, he was part owner in three turpentine distilleries, one of which had formerly been owned by Thomas S. Singleton. After Burnside's attack on New Bern in March 1862, Moore relocated to Charlotte, North Carolina, where he resided until April 1865. An advertisement in Capt. R. A. Shotwell's 1866 New Bern city directory listed Moore as the vice-president and a director of the National Bank of New Bern. Significantly, Moore was appointed to New Bern's slave patrol in 1845 and seems to have been a slave trader as

well. Singleton would have resided at the Gaston House from about 1855 to 1858, and evidence suggests that he could have been sold while living there. In 1856, Moore sold thirty-nine slaves for a total of twenty-two thousand dollars to neighbors Alexander Mitchell and Isaac M. Hughes. Included in this transaction was a slave known as "William Henry." Instead of being called the "Don't know" boy, Singleton could have dropped his surname and simply been known as William Henry. If Mitchell and Hughes did purchase Singleton, he probably would have remained in New Bern as both were local residents and Hughes was part owner of a local turpentine distillery. Perhaps they even hired him out and he continued to work at the hotel. It is possible that Moore knew that Singleton was a fugitive and might have used this knowledge to his own advantage. One doubts that Moore's scruples prevented him from taking advantage of Singleton's labor, even if he knew that the slave belonged to John H. Nelson. On the other hand, Singleton could have managed to escape detection as a fugitive slave by blending into the state's largest free black population. By 1860, approximately one of every four African Americans living in New Bern was free. Watson mentions the Gaston House Hotel in his *History of New Bern and Craven County*, see 306, 417, 514, and especially 358. Peter Sandbeck discusses the influence of the turpentine industry in New Bern in *The Historic Architecture of New Bern and Craven County, North Carolina* (New Bern, N.C.: Tryon Palace Commission, 1988), 95-96, 100. See also David M. Dudley (for Hughes and Dudley) and William P. Moore, New Bern Town Taxables Records, 1848, 1849. Regarding William P. Moore, see Craven County Miscellaneous Records, Slaves and Free Negroes, NCSA; William P. Moore, October 16, 1856, Book 64, p. 145, Craven County Deeds, RDO-NB; William P. Moore, Applications for Pardon, Craven County, N.C., Military Collection, Civil War Collection, NCSA; R. A. Shotwell, *New Bern Mercantile and Manufacturers' Business Directory and N.C. Farmer's Reference Book* (New Bern: W. I. Vestal, 1866). For population figures, see U.S. Bureau of the Census, *Statistics of the United States in 1860, Compiled from the Original Returns and Being the Final Exhibit of the Eighth Census* (Washington, D.C.: Government Printing Office, 1866), 349, 351, 355, 359.

28. Born in 1814, John H. Nelson would have been forty-seven years old at the start of the war. Carraway, *South River*, 51.

29. As previously noted, Edward H. Nelson (1842-1877), second son of John H. and Eliza Hall Nelson, is listed as nineteen in the 1860 federal census and so was about the same age as Singleton. 1860 Census: Craven County, N.C., Population Schedule.

30. Long after the Civil War, local lore held up the John H. Nelson house at Garbacon Creek as a site of notorious brutality against slaves. Dollie C. Carraway, a local historian who lives near Garbacon Creek, has noted: "[O]n the top floor of the house was a room with a big post set up in the middle of it. It was here that the slaves were whipped when they disobeyed the master of the farm. It was called the 'Whipping Post.' As long as the old house was standing, there were stains on the floor around the post and on the stairs, made from the blood dropped from the whipped slaves." Carraway's aunt lived in the Nelson house during the 1920s and reported to her niece that she and another relative had tried unsuccessfully to wash away the stains. Carraway, *South River*, 51.

31. As discussed in note 2, Singleton is mistaken about the identity of his father. John H. Nelson's only brother, Benjamin F., died shortly after their father in 1833, a full ten years before Singleton's birth. Benjamin received medical attention as late as November 28 but was dead the next day. Samuel Hyman, the executor of his estate, paid John Court $9.50 for the hire of African American boatman Joseph Delamar and three hands to carry the body across Adams Creek to its burial place. Benjamin F. Nelson was laid to rest in a mahogany coffin with a silver plate and black velvet trimming. Will of Benjamin F. Nelson, 1833, Craven County Wills, NCSA; Estate of Benjamin F. Nelson, 1833, Craven County Estates Records, NCSA.

32. Based on the division of slaves according to John S. Nelson's 1833 estate records, the slaves Pleasant and/or Betty could be the aunt to whom Singleton refers. Pleasant was an infant in 1833 and was included with her mother, Comfort, in Lot #1, drawn by Ester E. Nelson. Pleasant would have been in her early twenties around the time this comment was made. Betty, who was sixteen years old in 1833, and her infant, Caroline,

were part of Lot #5, drawn by Susan T. Nelson. Susan Nelson wed James G. Stanly Jr. in 1834. Estate of John S. Nelson, 1833, Craven County Estates Records, NCSA; Craven County Marriage Bonds, NCSA; Carraway, *South River*, 48.

33. The Nelsons had six daughters, only three of whom survived childhood. Most likely, the eldest, Susan J., born in 1844 and closest to Singleton in age, made this comment. The other daughters included Francis Love, born in 1846, and Cora L., born in 1852. Carraway, *South River*, 48, 53-54; 1850 and 1860 Censuses: Craven County, N.C., Population Schedules.

34. As pointed out earlier, according to available marriage records, no John Singleton ever married a Nelson in Craven County. Singleton is referring to Eliza A. Hall who married John H. Nelson in October 1835. She was seventeen years old at the time. Her parents, John and Love Hall, lived on a tract of land known as Sand Hills located on the east side of Garbacon Creek, between Herring Pond and South River. Craven County Marriage Bonds, NCSA; Carraway, *South River*, 48, 53-54.

35. There was a "Frank, age 12" listed among John S. Nelson's slaves when he died in 1833. Frank, like Lettice, was included in Lot #2 when Nelson's slaves were divided and was drawn by son John H. Nelson. Frank would have been about the same age as Lettice. Slave schedules indicate one female, age 27, and one male, age 30, were among the slaves on the John H. Nelson plantation in 1850. These are the only slaves of approximately the correct age and gender that appear. By 1860, when Lettice and Frank would have been about thirty-eight years old, Nelson listed one male and one female, both age thirty-five. Again, these are the closest to Frank and Lettice in age on the list. Estate of John S. Nelson, 1833, Craven County Estates Records, NCSA; 1850 and 1860 Censuses: Craven County, N.C., Slave Schedules.

36. Eliza Hall Nelson died January 28, 1860, and was buried at the Hall-Nelson cemetery between Herring Pond and the South River, approximately five miles from the Nelson plantation. Carraway, *South River*, 48, 56. Given the rising tensions over slavery and the increasing intolerance toward abolitionist sentiment within the South just prior to

the Civil War, Eliza's comments would have indeed caused quite a stir on the Nelson plantation. While plantation mistresses wielded power within the domestic sphere, they were expected to remain silent on the issue of slavery. With these few words, Eliza Nelson challenged her husband's absolute authority as head of the patriarchal social order. At the same time, the impression that they would have made on the slaves guaranteed that Eliza would be well remembered in posterity. Clinton, *Plantation Mistress*, 179, 181-183, 187, 188, 192.

37. John H. Nelson married twenty-five-year-old Mehetible "Hettie" N. Mason of Adams Creek on March 26, 1860. She died September 27, 1917, and is buried next to her husband in Beaufort, N.C. Craven County Marriage Bonds, NCSA; Carraway, *South River*, 50.

38. Eugene Genovese has argued that many slaveholders did indeed view their slaves as being better off than northern industrial workers. Genovese, *Roll, Jordan, Roll*, 57-63.

39. Militant abolitionist John Brown (1800-1859) led the unsuccessful raid on the federal arsenal at Harpers Ferry, Virginia, on October 16, 1859. Captured by Colonel Robert E. Lee, Brown was tried two weeks later and sentenced to hang on December 2, 1859. In the minds of southern slaveholders, Harpers Ferry proved that the abolitionists would stop at nothing and strengthened their resolve to preserve the southern way of life at all costs. *The National Cyclopædia of American Biography*, vol. 2 (New York: James T. White and Company, 1921), 307-08; Oakes, *The Ruling Race*, 233-34. For a good firsthand account of the Underground Railroad, see William Still, *The Underground Railroad: A Record of Facts, Authentic Narratives, Letters, etc., Narrating the Hardships, Hair-Breadth Escapes, and Death Struggles of the Slaves in Their Efforts for Freedom* (Philadelphia: Porter and Coates, 1872).

40. Singleton's allusion to the complex class relations in the antebellum South makes an important point: many poor whites did sympathize with slaves and frequently assisted fugitives. At the same time, the nature of the paternalistic social order also tended to generate hostility between slaves and lower-class whites. On sympathy between slaves and poor

whites, see Cecelski, "Shores of Freedom," especially n. 46. For tension, see Genovese, *Roll, Jordan, Roll,* 22-25.

41. William Lloyd Garrison (1805-1879) and Wendell Phillips (1811-1884) were two of the most preeminent white abolitionists. In 1831, Garrison, a journalist, formed the New England Anti-Slavery Society and began publishing his newspaper, the *Liberator,* which quickly became one of the most vocal organs of the abolition movement. Lawyer Wendell Phillips joined the movement in 1835 after seeing Garrison dragged through the streets of Boston and beaten for his antislavery beliefs. He soon became a chief spokesman for the "Garrisonian" abolitionists. Unlike other groups, such as the American Anti-Slavery Society, Garrison and his followers refuted gradualism and colonization schemes and called for an immediate end to slavery. *National Cyclopædia of American Biography,* 2:305-306, 314-315.

42. "Colonel Nelson" is Wiley M. Nelson (1794-1856), the cousin who lived next to the John H. Nelson plantation and owned thirty-two slaves. Wiley Nelson also owned a considerable amount of property in New Bern, including two improved lots. One was next door to Thomas S. Singleton's residence on Johnson Street (between Hancock and Middle Streets), and the other was next door to Spyers Singleton Smith (grandson to the original Spyers Singleton) on Graves Street. Nelson appears to have divided his time between his residences in New Bern and his plantation near Garbacon Creek. Upon his death, Wiley Nelson not only freed his slaves in his will but also provided for their travel expenses to Liberia. Relatives contested Colonel Nelson's will, but the North Carolina Supreme Court upheld it, and on May 1, 1858, all of his former slaves sailed for Africa. Wiley M. Nelson is buried in the Cedar Grove Cemetery in New Bern. Wiley M. Nelson, New Bern Town Taxables Records, 1840, 1842, 1845-1846, 1849; Carraway, *South River,* 99. For information pertaining to Nelson manumitting his slaves, see Memory F. Mitchell, "Off to Africa—With Judicial Blessing," *NCHR* 53 (summer 1976): 279-282.

43. Camp meetings were not only an integral part of the spiritual life of many North Carolina communities but also a much-anticipated form of

recreation. Baptists, Methodists, and Presbyterians all sponsored camp meetings, usually as part of week-long revivals. Such gatherings attracted large crowds and allowed friends and neighbors time off from work to visit with each other. Preachers and exhorters relied on singing to set the tone of the service throughout and often emphasized egalitarian themes in their sermons. For an excellent discussion of camp meetings, see Johnson, *Ante-Bellum North Carolina*, 100, 371-409. In 1884 a correspondent to the *New Berne Journal* reminisced about life at Adams Creek in the 1850s. Among his general references were the "Old Winthrop farm" and Mrs. Nelson's old windmill at Smith's Creek. Particularly, he recalled an "Adams Creek camp meeting" and its "leading spirits," John H. Nelson, Nelson's cousins Colonel Wiley M. Nelson and James F. Nelson, and his father-in-law, Francis Mason. *New Berne Journal*, August 21, 1884; Carraway, *South River*, 48.

44. Traveling preacher Peter Howell noted the Nelson family's religious devotion when he recorded in his journal that he "[s]upped with Brother Nelson from Adams Creek in New Bern on July 23, 1848." *The Life and Travels of Peter Howell, Written By Himself* (New Bern, N.C.: W. H. Mayhew, 1849), 287.

45. A presiding elder served as a superintendent in charge of the spiritual and temporal well-being of the church in his appointed district. Duties included traveling and preaching throughout his district, overseeing the work of the local preachers in the absence of the bishop, and presiding over the quarterly conference. As much as his time would allow, the presiding elder was also required to attend all quarterly meetings. John J. Tigert, ed., *The Doctrines and Discipline of the Methodist Episcopal Church, South* (Nashville, Tenn.: Barbee and Smith, 1898), 54-56.

46. Singleton apparently conflates this local incident, which "could not have been so very long before the beginning of the war," and the official break between the North and the South in the Methodist Episcopal Church, which occurred much earlier, in 1844. The suspensions of Bishop James O. Andrew of Georgia, who had inherited two slaves through marriage, and minister Francis A. Harding, also a slaveholder,

emerged as the central issues of that year's general conference and underlined the growing division between North and South. The immediate question before the conference was should bishops of the church "in any manner" be "implicated with slavery." Bishop Andrew willingly resigned as requested, and Harding was suspended. When Harding appealed, 117 ministers voted to uphold his suspension, while only 56 voted to rescind it. Conference members had long viewed slavery as evil and had even defined it as such in their *Discipline*, but they diverged on what the church's official position with regard to slavery should be. Those in the North viewed the issue as an inherently moral and ethical one, whereas those in the South tended to see slavery as a civil and political dilemma, and therefore outside ecclesiastical jurisdiction. Nonetheless, southerners found it impossible to support the unmistakably antislavery stance established during these proceedings. On June 5, 1844, A. B. Longstreet, also of Georgia, declared, "[T]he continued agitation on the subject of slavery and abolition in a portion of the church . . . and especially the extra-judicial proceedings against Bishop Andrew . . . renders a continuance of the jurisdiction of this General Conference . . . inconsistent with the success of the ministry in the slaveholding states." Soon afterward, the southern conferences adopted the Plan of Separation in which they announced their intention to form a separate organization known as the Methodist Episcopal Church, South. Leaders met in Louisville in May 1845 to organize their new church and held their first general conference a year later in Virginia. After the official break in the church, tensions continued to build between the two factions, with each side claiming divine sanction for its point of view. They would not be reunified until 1939. *The General Conferences of the Methodist Episcopal Church from 1792-1896* (New York: Eaton and Mains, 1900); *The History of American Methodism in Three Volumes*, vol. 2 (New York: Abingdon Press, 1964), 50-70, 145-147, 155, 157.

47. Founded in 1788 and originally known as the Adams Creek Methodist Episcopal Church, the church is today known as the Merrimon United Methodist Church and is one of the oldest church congregations in North Carolina. The church building is located at the

intersection of Merrimon and South River Roads on the east side of Adams Creek. Carraway, *South River*, 105-107.

48. Methodist Church records do not indicate a presiding elder or minister by the name of Ayers in antebellum North Carolina. William Closs was the presiding elder of the New Bern District from 1847 to 1850 until David B. Nicholson took the post and served from 1851 to 1853. Ira S. Wyde presided from 1854 to1857, followed by Closs who resumed his former duties from 1858 to 1861. In 1854, the New Bern district had 3,323 white and 2,681 black congregants. The New Bern circuit, or smaller society located around the principal district, comprised 195 whites and 119 blacks. By 1860, there were 4,450 Methodists worshiping in fifteen churches in Craven County. *Minutes of the Annual Conferences of the Methodist Episcopal Church, South* (Raleigh, N.C.: Methodist Episcopal Conference, published annually for the years 1845-1865); Methodist Episcopal Church, Conferences, *Minutes of the Annual Conferences* (Raleigh, N.C.: Methodist Episcopal Conference, published annually); Osmon C. Baker, *A Guide-Book in the Administration of the Discipline of the Methodist Episcopal Church* (New York: Carlton and Phillips, 1855), 38-39; U.S. Bureau of the Census, *Statistics of the U.S. in 1860*, 437. It is possible that John H. Nelson purchased Ennis Delamar from the Delamars who lived opposite Garbacon Creek on the north side of the Neuse River. In 1850, thirty-year-old farmer Stephen Delamar owned eleven slaves and lived at Bay River. His kinsman and neighbor William Delamar, age forty, also owned eleven slaves.

The anonymous correspondent to the *New Berne Journal* also recalled a camp meeting at Bryant's Pond and wondered what had become of William and Stephen Delamar and their neighbors. What became of Ennis Delamar after the war remains unclear as he does not appear in the 1870 census. *New Berne Journal*, August 21, 1884; 1850, 1860, and 1870 Censuses: Craven County, N.C., Population Schedules, and 1850 and 1860 Slave Schedules.

49. The Bible verse Ennis Delamar alluded to in his prayer is "Princes shall come out of Egypt; Ethiopia shall soon stretch out her hands unto God." Psalms 68:31, King James Version (hereafter cited as KJV).

50. For a presiding elder to direct some of his attention toward the slaves would not have been unusual, as Methodist ministers had long endeavored to address the spiritual needs of enslaved men and women in their mission work. They preached to the slaves who sat in the balcony at their master's church and visited slaves to administer the sacrament and baptize their children. Did Singleton's master have the power to defy church authority by sending the presiding elder on his way? According to the Methodist *Discipline,* "a Presiding Elder may remove a preacher from his charge" but not vice versa. At the same time, the ministers of the Methodist Episcopal Church, South, had formally deemed slavery beyond the jurisdiction of ecclesiastical authority. Informally, then, southern ministers were bound by their congregation's support of slavery. Though they might not have condoned it personally, they could not speak out against it publicly without risking their jobs. See "Presiding Elders," in Baker, *Guide-Book in the Administration of the Discipline of the Methodist Episcopal Church,* 58; *The History of American Methodism,* 2:157.

51. Samuel Hyman Jr. was John H. Nelson's nephew, son of his sister Mary and Samuel Hyman. Student records indicate that no one named Hyman either graduated or entered classes at West Point from 1851 to 1860. Hyman could have been enrolled in a military academy elsewhere. Wherever he had been, on the eve of the Civil War, the twenty-one-year-old Hyman was living at the New Bern Hotel. Hyman probably asked his uncle John H. Nelson for a manservant to accompany him. At the time of his death, Samuel Hyman Sr. owned twenty-four slaves. Records indicate that these slaves were to be hired out until his four children came of age, but by 1850, only nine remained as part of the estate. In 1860, Samuel Hyman Jr. owned four slaves: two males, ages 50 and 2, and two females, ages 32 and 8, whom he mortgaged to Charles C. Clark. Due to their gender and ages, these slaves could not have gone with the young Hyman to war. It was also about this time that Singleton's mother became involved with Arne[s]t Nelson, and the changes in the household might have been uncomfortable for William Henry, thereby increasing his willingness to accompany Hyman. Index of Cadets, West Point Museum, West Point Military Academy, N.Y.;

"Account of the Slaves belonging to John, Samuel, Margaret and Eliza Hyman, January 1, 1850," Estate of Samuel Hyman, 1843, Craven County Estates Records, NCSA; 1860 Census: Craven County, N.C., Population and Slave Schedules; Samuel O. Hyman, August 17, 1860, Book 66, p.137, Craven County Deeds, RDO-NB.

52. Confederate troops fired on Fort Sumter, South Carolina, on April 12, 1861. Private Samuel O. Hyman belonged to Company K., Second Regiment, North Carolina State Troops, also called the "Elm City Rifles." A Craven County resident, he enlisted at New Bern on June 21, 1861. Private Hyman was with the regiment continuously until his death at Chancellorsville, Virginia, on May 3, 1863. Louis H. Manarin and Weymouth T. Jordan Jr., comps., *North Carolina Troops, 1861-1865: A Roster*, 14 vols. to date (Raleigh: Division of Archives and History, Department of Cultural Resources, 1966-), 3:470, 474 (hereafter cited as *NC Troops*).

53. Apparently Hyman's unit did not fight at the Battle of New Bern but was nearby at Goldsboro on March 25, 1862. On April 30, they were ordered to Wilmington. Manarin and Jordan, *NC Troops*, 3:372.

Ambrose Everett Burnside (1824-1881) graduated from West Point in 1847. After the first Battle of Bull Run he became a brigadier general and after New Bern was promoted to major general. Burnside accepted the post of commander of the Army of the Potomac in November 1862. Lincoln relieved him of his duties in January 1863, shortly after Fredericksburg. Burnside then assumed command of the Army of Ohio and fought at the siege of Knoxville. Following the war, he served as governor of Rhode Island and as a U.S. senator. John Gray Foster (1823-1874) graduated from West Point in 1846. When the Civil War began he was appointed as head engineer in charge of fortifying Charleston Harbor. Foster commanded the New England Brigade, including the Tenth Connecticut, at Roanoke Island and New Bern. In March 1864, Foster assumed command of the Department of the South and assisted Sherman in Savannah and Charleston. Following the war, Foster returned to New England where he worked as an engineer. On Burnside, see Mark Mayo Boatner III, *The Civil War Dictionary*, rev. ed. (New York: David McKay Company, 1988), 107-108; on Foster, see

John T. Hubbell and James W. Geary, *Biographical Dictionary of the Union, Northern Leaders of the Civil War* (Westport, Conn.: Greenwood Press, 1995), 182.

The Battle of New Bern began early in the morning of March 14, 1862. Confederate general L. O'B. Branch's four thousand men, comprising the 7th, 26th, 27th, 33rd, 35th, and 37th North Carolina State Troops, faced General Ambrose E. Burnside's eleven thousand troops and were in retreat to Kinston by mid-afternoon. Kinston is thirty miles from New Bern by rail. The loss of New Bern was a severe blow to the Confederates because of the city's importance as a port and its position along the Atlantic and North Carolina Railroad. Not long after Union officials restored order to the town, Burnside appointed General John G. Foster as military governor of the city. Over the next several months, Burnside was periodically absent from New Bern but continued to use it as his headquarters until he left on July 6, 1862, to assist George E. McClellan's Army of the Potomac in Virginia. *OR*, ser. 1, 9:196-270; Barrett, *Civil War in North Carolina*, 95-108, 209.

54. Burnside actually had two headquarters in New Bern. The first, known as the Charles Slover House, was located at the southwest corner of Union and East Front Streets, facing the Neuse River. The second was the John Wright Stanly House located at the southwest corner of New and Middle Streets, with its entrance on Middle Street. Burnside occupied both sites by mid-1862, and Singleton could be referring to either. An 1862 map of New Bern was printed in James A. Emmerton's *A Record of the Twenty-third Regiment Mass. Vol. Infantry* (Boston, Mass.: William Ware and Company, 1886). Singleton was not alone in his effort to escape to the Union lines in New Bern. At least ten thousand slaves fled to the city and other Federally occupied towns along the North Carolina coast. Burnside described the dilemma the runaways presented in a letter to Secretary of War Edwin M. Stanton dated March 21, 1862: "They are now a source of very great anxiety to us. The city is being overrun with fugitives from the surrounding towns and plantations. . . . It would be utterly impossible, if we were so disposed, to keep them outside of our lines, as they find their way to us through woods and swamps from every side." *OR*, ser. 1, 9:199.

55. Lieutenant Colonel Robert Leggett of New London enlisted as a captain in the Tenth Connecticut Infantry Regiment, Company K, on April 29, 1861. After being mustered in on October 1, the regiment joined Burnside at Roanoke Island, N.C., on February 8, 1862. Following his service in New Bern, Lieutenant Colonel Leggett saw action at Morris Island, South Carolina, in July 1863 and was discharged on August 17, 1864. *Record of the Service of Connecticut Men in the Army & Navy of the United States During the War of the Rebellion* (Hartford, Conn.: Press of the Case, Lockwood, Brainard, 1889), 398, 420. Copy at the New Haven Colony Historical Society, New Haven, Conn.

56. The "First North Carolina Calvary" was the First Regiment, North Carolina Calvary, and was officially designated the Ninth Regiment, North Carolina State Troops. The regiment was organized at Camp Beauregard, Ridgeway, Warren County, on August 12, 1861, and was one of three regiments ordered back home from Virginia when Burnside's expedition threatened the state in early 1862. The Ninth North Carolina went into Camp Ransom in Kinston in April 1862 and remained there until called back piecemeal to Virginia by the end of June. There was no Major Richardson in the Ninth North Carolina, but Singleton could have been referring to a number of men. He most likely meant Private George A. Richardson, Company C, Eighth Battalion North Carolina Partisan Rangers. Private Richardson was captured December 14, 1862, and paroled at New Bern on December 23, 1862. Federal soldiers characterized the Partisan Rangers as Confederate "guerrillas." For information on the Ninth North Carolina State Troops and Private George Richardson, see Manarin and Jordan, *NC Troops*, 2:607. For information on guerrillas, see Barrett, *Civil War in North Carolina*, 173, 179-181.

57. Singleton is referring to Wise Forks, a small community in northwest Jones County, approximately five miles south of Kinston. Powell, *North Carolina Gazetteer*, 540.

58. Vincent Coyler describes a similar incident in which Sam Williams, a freedman of New Bern, aided Foster in planning an expedition by mapping out routes over land and through swamps. In this particular

case, the commanding officer chose an alternate route and as a result the Rebels were able to hold their ground. The colonel later admitted that if he had followed Williams's advice, the expedition would have been a success. Vincent Coyler, *A Brief Report of the Services Rendered by the Freed People to the U.S. Army in North Carolina, In the Spring of 1862, After the Battle of New Bern* (New York: Vincent Coyler, 1864), 24-25.

59. Singleton could be talking about a number of skirmishes here. Since he worked for Lieutenant Colonel Leggett, whose Second Brigade fell under Foster's command, it is likely that he did participate in various attacks while he was based in occupied New Bern. On April 20, 1862, Burnside reported to Stanton that "General Foster . . . is pushing his outposts in the direction of Kinston as rapidly as the present force will admit." Wise Forks is located at the intersection of Dover and Upper Trent Roads, the latter following the course of the Trent River. Not incidentally, Private Samuel O. Hyman's regiment, the Second North Carolina Infantry, had been stationed at Wise Forks since April 13, and on April 27 there was a "severe but undecisive skirmish" in the area. Union expeditions also left New Bern and moved toward Kinston in June, November, and December 1862. In all, they fought four battles and were involved in numerous skirmishes along the Neuse River and the Atlantic and North Carolina Railroad line nearby. Leaving New Bern on December 10, Foster's troops succeeded in capturing Kinston on the fourteenth, but only after losing between 300 and 400 men. The victory was short-lived. The Confederates recaptured Kinston, and throughout the rest of the war, the area around Kinston was one of contention between Union and Confederate troops. On March 8, 1865, Rebels managed to delay the Union advance on Kinston at the Battle of Wise Forks, but only for a few days. Barrett provides an excellent description of the location of Wise Forks and the 1865 battle. Barrett, *Civil War in North Carolina*, 285-290. For Foster's advances, see *OR*, ser. 1, 9:124-125, 273, 298-303, 372-373, 389, 415; ser. 1, 13:84; Robert A. Campbell, *The Rebellion Register* (Kalamazoo, Mich.: R.A. Campbell, 1866), 186-187.

60. Andrew's Chapel had been the home of New Bern's black Methodists since 1838. The church was originally located on Hancock Street, between South Front and Pollock Streets. In the midst of the Civil

War, the A.M.E. Zion church at New Haven led the New England Conference's effort to establish a church in the rebelling states. Shortly after the arrival of Bishop J. W. Hood in New Bern on January 24, 1864, Andrew's Chapel, with a membership of four hundred, became the first official A.M.E. Zion church in the South. For three years Hood remained as pastor of the New Bern church, which was renamed Saint Peter's. Hood, *One Hundred Years*, 290-293; *History of American Methodism*, 2:560; Watson, *History of New Bern and Craven County*, 413. John L. Bell Jr. provides an insightful sketch of the life of Bishop Hood, an African American, who resided in North Carolina for the rest of his life and was a political activist throughout Reconstruction. See Powell, *Dictionary of North Carolina*, 3:195-196.

61. The drilling activities of Singleton's makeshift regiment caused much consternation among some Union officers in New Bern. Not only did they object because Lincoln had not approved black military service, but they also discovered that the black soldiers refused impressment into the work gangs that built fortifications and performed a variety of other jobs. In a February 19, 1863, letter to his headquarters, Lieutenant George F. Woodman, the deputy provost marshal of the Eighteenth Army Corps in New Bern, acknowledged that he had sought confirmation from his superiors that, "no authority had been given to any person or persons to raise a Negro regiment." He reported that the black men had begun drilling after "one colored man," presumably Singleton, "had been told that if he procured the names of one thousand colored men, who were willing to enlist as soldiers, their services might be accepted." The provost marshal arrested "about one hundred negros" until they agreed to be impressed into work gangs. Lieutenant George F. Woodman to Lieutenant Colonel Hoffman, February 19, 1863, in Ira Berlin, Joseph P. Reidy, Leslie Rowland, eds., *Freedom: A Documentary History of Emancipation, 1861-1867—Series 2: The Black Military Experience* (Cambridge: Cambridge University Press, 1993), 129.

62. Lincoln did not visit New Bern during the Civil War, thus Singleton's encounter with the president could have only occurred on July 9, 1862, at Burnside's headquarters at Fort Monroe, Virginia. Burnside departed

from North Carolina on July 6, under orders to assist General McClellan's Army of the Potomac, which was then stationed along the James River at Camp Near, Harrison's Landing, Virginia. Shortly after his arrival at Fort Monroe on the afternoon of July 7, Burnside received a message from the secretary of war. Stanton wrote: "The President is on the way to meet you at Fort Monroe. Please remain, and do not send your troops forward until you meet him." Around five o'clock the next day, Lincoln reviewed McClellan's troops at Camp Near. It seems Lincoln met with Burnside the next day, on July 9. In a letter to McClellan's assistant adjutant-general dated July 10, Major General John A. Dix, also at Fort Monroe, mentioned Stanton's earlier dispatch and noted that after Lincoln's return to Washington "last evening," he had given the order for the transportation of the troops. Singleton is ambiguous about how long he was away from New Bern with Burnside. However, he later claims that he had returned home by the time Lincoln signed the Emancipation Proclamation on January 1, 1863, raising the possibility that he was with Burnside for nearly six months. Stanton's message to Burnside appears in *OR*, ser. 1, 9:409. To follow Lincoln's trail, see *OR*, ser. 1, 11:305, 307, 311.

63. James Chaplain Beecher (1828-1886) was serving as a missionary to China at the beginning of the Civil War. He assumed command of the Thirty-fifth U.S.C.T. on May 18, 1863. At the end of the war, he resumed his work in the ministry and later committed suicide. Congregationalist minister Henry Ward Beecher was a leading antislavery speaker who criticized Lincoln for not advocating the abolition of slavery from the war's inception. "Beecher's Bibles," Sharps carbines and rifles shipped to Kansas in a crate labeled "Bibles," took their name from the militant minister, who claimed that when it came to southern slaveholders, he saw "more moral power in one of those instruments . . . than in a hundred bibles." After the war, Beecher supported extending the franchise to African Americans and women. The Beechers were brothers to Harriet Beecher Stowe, author of *Uncle Tom's Cabin*. Stewart Sifakis, *Who Was Who in the Civil War* (New York: Facts on File Publications, 1988), 46; Hubbell and Geary, *Biographical Dictionary of the Union*, 33-34; Boatner, *Civil War Dictionary*, 56. On April 1, 1863, John A. Andrew,

abolitionist governor of Massachusetts, informed Stanton that, with regard to the organization of African American troops, he had "information leading me to the belief that . . . good troops can be raised in North Carolina in numbers from 2,500 to 5,000 now within General Foster's lines." As noted in the introduction, Foster was ambivalent at best regarding the enlistment of African Americans. Two weeks later, on May 18, Colonel Edward A. Wild, of the Thirty-fifth Massachusetts, arrived in New Bern to begin recruiting soldiers for his "African Brigade." Significantly, blacks who had been employed as laborers, like Singleton, emerged as leaders in drilling exercises. For communications from Andrew and Foster to Stanton, see *OR*, ser. 3, 3:109-110, 192. For a thoroughly insightful discussion of "Wild's Brigade," see Richard Reid's "Raising the African Brigade: Early Black Recruitment in Civil War North Carolina," *NCHR* 70 (July 1993): 266-301.

64. Official records indicate that William Henry Singleton enlisted in the Union army on May 27, 1863, and served as sergeant of Company G, Thirty-fifth U.S.C.T. for the remainder of the war. By June 1, Company G contained ninety-two men. See Descriptive Books of the Thirty-fifth, Thirty-sixth, and Thirty-seventh Regiments of the United States Colored Troops, NCSA; Henry Singleton, Declaration for Pension, April 9, 1898, NA; *Personal War Sketches of the Admiral Foote Post, No. 17, Department of Connecticut, Grand Army of the Republic* (New Haven, Conn., 1890), 66. Original copy at the New Haven Colony Historical Society. See also Reid, "Raising the African Brigade," 287. The first African Americans were mustered into the Union army in Louisiana on September 27, 1862. The First South Carolina Volunteers followed on January 31, 1863. Though Singleton's regiment was not the first, records indicate that by October 31, 1863, Colonel J. C. Beecher commanded 1,002 men. *OR*, ser. 3, 3:1115; ser. 3, 5:660-662. Singleton took an active role in pressing the federal government to accept African Americans into service. Abraham Galloway, a former fugitive slave and Union spy, led a movement in New Bern to ensure fair treatment for black soldiers after enlistment. The freedmen who had already organized themselves into military drilling units, like Singleton, made their way to the recruiting office only after Colonel Edward A. Wild's emissary acceded

to their demands, which included equal pay and protection for their families. He did so without authorization, as Galloway's men held a revolver to his head. David S. Cecelski, "Abraham Galloway: Wilmington's Lost Prophet and the Origins of Black Radicalism in the South," in *Democracy Betrayed: The Wilmington Race Riot of 1898 and Its Legacy,* ed. David S. Cecelski and Timothy B. Tyson (Chapel Hill: University of North Carolina Press, 1998), 43-72.

65. Josiah C. White, originally of Boston, was appointed captain of the Thirty-fifth U.S.C.T. on April 28, 1863. He was wounded in the Battle of Honey Hill on November 3, 1864. Reid also notes that Captain White was one of Wild's enrolling officers in Beaufort County. "List of Commissioned Officers, 35th Regiment," Descriptive Books of Thirty-fifth, Thirty-sixth, and Thirty-seventh Regiments of the United States Colored Troops, NCSA; Reid, "Raising the African Brigade," 280. Pennsylvania native Joseph E. Williams, also a member of Wild's Brigade, noted that by late June 1863 the black women of New Bern had ordered a battle flag for Singleton's regiment. He described it as "made of blue silk, with a yellow silk fringe. . . . On one side the Goddess of Liberty is represented with her right foot resting on a copperhead snake. On the reverse side, a large gilt rising sun, with the word 'Liberty' in very large letters over the sun." Edwin S. Redkey, ed., *A Grand Army of Black Men: Letters from African American Soldiers in the Union Army, 1861-1865* (New York: Cambridge University Press, 1992), 91.

66. The First North Carolina Colored Infantry was redesignated the Thirty-fifth U.S. Colored Troops on February 8, 1864. Except for occasional raids in South Carolina, the regiment mainly saw action in Florida as a part of Montgomery's Brigade. They were ordered to Charleston, S.C., in March 1865. The Thirty-fifth U.S.C.T. lost a total of 205 men during the war. Frederick H. Dyer, *A Compendium of the War of the Rebellion,* vol. 3, *Regimental Histories* (New York: Thomas Yoselhoff, 1959), 1729.

67. On February 20, 1864, Union troops suffered heavy casualties, 37.5 percent of their men, in an unsuccessful attempt to sever the railroad link between east and west Florida at the Suwannee River. The Battle of

Olustee claimed the lives of 2 officers and 20 men of the Thirty-fifth U.S.C.T., with 8 officers and 123 men wounded and 77 men reported missing at the end of the day. According to Brigadier General T. Seymour, the "First North Carolina fought like veterans." Recalling the battle three years later, William Wells Brown celebrated the men of the Fifty-fourth Massachusetts and the First North Carolina, both African American regiments, for saving the day at Olustee. William Wells Brown, *The Negro in the American Rebellion*, annotated by William Edward Farrison (New York: Citadel Press, 1971), 217-224; *OR*, ser. 1, 35, pt. 1:288-200, 208. One extant personal war sketch for Singleton states that he was wounded in the left leg in the Battle of Honey Hill, which occurred on November 30, 1864, near Grahamville, South Carolina. *Personal War Sketches of the Admiral Foote Post, No. 17*, 66. For information on Honey Hill, see *OR*, ser. 1, 44:426-427.

68. Singleton first appears in the New Haven city directory in 1871. That same year he is listed as a trustee of the local A.M.E. Zion church. Organized as an independent black church in 1820, the Zion church in New Haven is the oldest African American church in that city. Bishop J. W. Hood, who later went to New Bern, served as its pastor in 1857. The church moved from its original location on Dixwell Avenue to Foote Street in 1872 and was then called the Foote Street A.M.E. Zion Church. Frederick Douglass once addressed New Haven's African Americans in the church on Foote Street. The church has the additional distinction of being the site of Booker T. Washington's final public speech in 1915. In 1907, the church was renamed the Varick Memorial A.M.E. Zion Church in honor of James Varick (1768-1827), a prominent bishop in the A.M.E. Zion denomination. *Benam's Greater New Haven City Directory and Annual Advertiser* (New Haven, Conn.: J. H. Benam), vol. 32 (1871): 72, 335, and vol. 34 (1873): 115; Richard A. G. Foster, "Short History of Varick Memorial African Methodist Episcopal Zion Church New Haven, Conn.," *A.M.E. Zion Quarterly Review*, 56 (winter 1945-1946): 17-21; Powell, *Dictionary of North Carolina Biography*, 3:195; R. R. Wright, *The Bishops of the African Methodist Episcopal Church* (Nashville, Tenn.: A.M.E. Sunday School Union, 1963), 385.

69. Henry and Thomas R. Trowbridge were shipping merchants in New Haven. Their family's business, Henry Trowbridge Son's, was one of the largest shipping houses in New England and conducted an extensive trade with the West Indies. Older brother Henry (1836-1900) married Lucy Parker, who died in 1881. In 1877, Singleton went to work for Thomas R. (1839-1898), the more prominent son. At the age of nineteen, Thomas R. Trowbridge left New Haven to oversee the company's office in Trinidad. While there, he served as the U.S. consul from March 1863 until he returned home later that summer. Thomas R. ran unsuccessfully for mayor on the Republican ticket in 1886. A member of numerous civic societies, he contributed eleven hundred dollars toward the establishment of the New Haven Public Library and served as president of the Board of Aldermen and of the New Haven Colony Historical Society. Both men are buried in the family plot at New Haven's Grove Street Cemetery. Scrapbook of Thomas R. Trowbridge Jr., Trowbridge Family Papers, Manuscript and Archives Room, Sterling Memorial Library, Yale University, New Haven, Conn.; Francis Bacon Trowbridge, *The Trowbridge Genealogy: History of the Trowbridge Family in America* (New Haven, Conn.: Tuttle, Morehouse and Taylor, 1908), 104; *Benam's Greater New Haven City Directory*, vol. 38 (1877), 214.

70. A primary factor in Singleton's decision to settle in New Haven may have been the connection between that city's A.M.E. Zion church and Saint Peter's in New Bern. One reason the New England church fathers targeted New Bern for their first mission in the South was the influence of those in their ranks who still had ties in the area. For example, former Craven County resident Christopher Rush (1777-1872), who was appointed bishop in 1828, had migrated out of the area in the early nineteenth century and by the time of the war held a prominent position in the New England A.M.E. Zion Conference. As previously mentioned, Bishop J. W. Hood, who for a short time called New Haven home, was the missionary appointed to travel to New Bern to establish a Zion congregation there. Significantly, Hood had once been pastor of the A.M.E. Zion church that Singleton joined in New Haven. Moving from North Carolina to New Haven, Singleton possibly followed coastal trade routes, paths well-worn by an earlier generation of African American

migrants from New Bern. Prior to the Civil War, as Robert Warner has observed, an "exceptional group of artisans" had migrated out of New Bern, and their success in New Haven compelled other black New Bernians to follow. Immediately after the war, the group from New Bern formed a social organization in New Haven that was known as the North Carolina Club. R. R. Wright, *The Bishops of the African Methodist Episcopal Church*, 385; Robert Austin Warner, *New Haven Negroes: A Social History* (New Haven: Yale University Press, 1940), 125, 192. See also notes 60 and 67 in this section.

71. A corporal of the Forty-fourth Massachusetts, stationed at New Bern, revealed the extent of the determination of African American recruits to learn to read when he commented in a letter: "Some of the poor fellows lie behind their breastwork with a spelling book in one hand and a musket in the other." Reid, "Raising the African Brigade," 273. Vincent Coyler also confirms that during the Federal occupation of New Bern Union soldiers, with Foster's consent, conducted evening classes for local blacks until military governor Edward Stanly ordered the schools closed. Coyler, *Report of the Services Rendered by the Freed People to the U.S. Army*, 43-44.

72. Of the six Salter families living in the Garbacon Creek and Adams Creek neighborhood in 1850, David Salter, a twenty-five-year-old farmer, and Dempsey Salter, a fifty-three-year-old farmer, appear to have resided closest to the Nelson plantation. 1850 Census: Craven County, N.C., Population Schedule. 1870 and 1880 census data indicate that two of Singleton's brothers, Hardy and Joseph, lived on their own places nearby. See note 7 in this section.

73. In 1870, thirty-two-year-old turpentine distiller Thomas Wheeler resided with his wife in New Bern's Third Ward. A search of Craven County deeds failed to produce a transaction by Wheeler on behalf of Singleton. 1870 Census: Craven County, N.C., Population Schedule. It is important to note, however, that Singleton uses this episode to call attention to his business acumen by claiming that he had made a three hundred dollar profit.

74. According to Foster, Singleton may well have been the "most outstanding member" of the A.M.E. Zion church in New Haven. He also points out that Singleton was well respected by both African American and white residents in that town for more than fifty years. Foster, "Short History of Varick Memorial African Methodist Episcopal Zion Church," 20.

75. Singleton moved to Portland in 1899. He appears in the city directory as the Reverend William Henry Singleton until 1901. The local A.M.E. Zion church was a mission without a permanent address until 1914, when it became the Green Memorial A.M.E. Zion Church, located at 42 Sheridan Avenue. *Munjoy Hill Historic Guide* (Portland, Maine: Greater Portland Landmarks, 1992), 9; *Portland City Directory*, 1899-1903, Portland, Maine.

76. Singleton married Maria Wanton of Middletown, Conn., in 1868. In 1880 the couple moved to 426 Orchard Street, where they lived until Maria's death in 1898, after which Singleton moved to Maine. Unfortunately, the house is no longer standing. As her husband preached on Sunday evening, May 15, 1898, Maria Singleton suddenly collapsed and died in church. Henry Singleton, Declaration for Pension, January 25, 1929, NA; *Benam's Greater New Haven Directory*, vol. 41 (1880), 242; Maria Singleton Death Certificate, May 15, 1898, Connecticut State Department of Health, Bureau of Vital Statistics, NA; Maria Singleton, Medical Examiner's Report, May 16, 1898, Connecticut Superior Court Docs. for New Haven County, Inquests 1898-1899, New Haven Colony Historical Society.

77. William Henry and Maria's daughter, Lulu W. Singleton (1884-1956), married Collins L. Fitch (1882-1951) in 1905. At that time Fitch worked at the Yale dining hall. By 1910, he worked as a porter for a local New Haven hotel and later settled into a permanent job as a letter carrier. The Fitches had seven sons and one daughter: Collins Jr., William S., Harrison B., Leroy E., George M., Milton F., Jerome H., and Althea E. Their mother, Lulu Singleton Fitch, is buried in a family plot next to her mother in New Haven's Evergreen Cemetery. Grandson Leroy E. Fitch attributes Singleton's misnaming Lulu's husband to the

fact that the family resided on Charles Street in New Haven. Leroy E. Fitch, interview with Katherine Mellen Charron, New Haven, Conn., February 11, 1999, telephone interview with Katherine Mellen Charron, March 1, 1999; 1910 Census: New Haven County, Conn., Population Schedule; *Greater New Haven City Directory* (New Haven, Conn.: Price and Lee, 1904, 1905, 1910, 1920, 1938); "List of Automobiles For Funeral of Colonel Wm. Henry Singleton," and "Colonel Wm. Henry Singleton," file at Beecher and Bennett, Inc., Funeral Home, West Haven, Conn.

78. Singleton wedded Charlotte Hinman in 1899, during his tenure with the A.M.E. Zion mission in Portland. The Singletons relocated to New York City in 1903, and then moved to Peekskill, New York, in 1907. They returned to New York City in 1925. Charlotte Singleton died at age fifty-five in Harlem Hospital on January 13, 1926, and was buried three days later at Rossville Cemetery on Staten Island. Following the death of his second wife, Singleton returned to New Haven where, at the age of eighty-seven, he married fifty-three-year-old Mary K. Powell on September 2, 1929. They lived in New Haven, settling permanently at 207 Dixwell Avenue in 1935. Not surprisingly, the third Mrs. Singleton survived her husband, and returned to Staten Island to live with her daughter following Singleton's death in 1938. With regard to Singleton's second marriage, see Henry Singleton, Declaration for Pension, January 25, 1929, NA; Loethe [*sic*] Singleton, January 13, 1926, Standard Certificate of Death, Bureau of Records of the Department of Health of the City of New York, NA. For information on his last marriage, see William Henry Singleton and Mary K. Powell Marriage License, September 2, 1929, Connecticut State Department of Health, Bureau of Vital Statistics, NA; *Greater New Haven City Directory*, 1928, 1930-1938.

79. By 1902, Singleton was working in Portland as a teamster; he moved to New York City a year later. He and his wife Charlotte resided in Peekskill from 1907 to 1924. According to a local history of Peekskill, Rev. William Henry Singleton was one of the city's "most prominent and highly respected citizens," known for his "eloquent speaking," and frequently called upon to deliver addresses on "patriotic occasions." Chester A. Smith, *Peekskill, A Friendly Town: Its Historic Sites and Shrines:*

A Pictorial History of the City From 1654-1952 (Peekskill, N.Y.: Friendly Town Association, 1952), 166.

80. Apparently, Singleton first worked for Lillian E. LeBaron, a widow, whose house was located on East Main Street in Peekskill. George F. Clark was a local businessman who employed Singleton as a coachman. *Peekskill Directory,* 1905-1908, Peekskill, N.Y.

81. George W. Buchanan owned a Standard Oil Cloth factory in a nearby village. He was a leader in the Peekskill business community from 1910 to 1920. Singleton, an elderly man by this time, seems to have worked as a caretaker for Buchanan. His address in the 1924 city directory, 769 Elm Street, is the same as his employer's. *Peekskill Directory,* 1907, 1924.

82. Singleton joined the Admiral Foote Post, No. 17, Grand Army of the Republic, on October 6, 1883. He served as its assistant chaplain from 1893 to 1895. Singleton also served as treasurer of the Oriental Lodge, No. 15, in New Haven in 1882. Civil War Collection, Admiral Foote Post, No. 17 (G.A.R.), New Haven Colony Historical Society; *Benam's Greater New Haven Directory,* vol. 43 (1882), 453.

83. The Mount Olivet Baptist Church was organized informally in the spring of 1893 at the home of Jane Clayborne and officially incorporated as a religious body on May 2, 1901. Shortly after Singleton's arrival in Peekskill, the church purchased land in order to build a permanent sanctuary. Members began worshiping there in 1910. "Mount Olivet Baptist Church History," program from the sixty-eighth anniversary of Mt. Olivet Baptist Church, October 12-16, 1961, Peekskill Churches File, Colin Naylor Local History Archives Room, Peekskill Field Library, Peekskill, N.Y.

84. 2 Cor. 5:17 King James Version.

85. Ps.16:6 KJV.

Works Cited

Primary Sources

Miscellaneous

Civil War Collection, Admiral Foote Post, No. 17 (Grand Army of the Republic), New Haven Colony Historical Society, New Haven, Conn.

Connecticut Superior Court Docs. for New Haven County, 1780-1923, Inquests 1898-1899, New Haven Colony Historical Society, New Haven, Conn.

Index of Cadets, West Point Museum, West Point Military Academy, New York.

"Mount Olivet Baptist Church History," program of the sixty-eighth anniversary of Mt. Olivet Baptist Church, October 12-16, 1961, Peekskill Churches File, Colin Naylor Local History Archives Room, Peekskill Field Library, Peekskill, N.Y.

Singleton, Colonel William Henry, file at Beecher and Bennett, Inc., Funeral Home, West Haven, Conn.

Trowbridge Family Papers, Manuscript and Archives Room, Sterling Memorial Library, Yale University, New Haven, Conn.

National Archives, Washington, D.C.

Eighth Census of the United States, 1860: Beaufort, Craven, Jones, and New Hanover Counties, North Carolina, Agriculture, Population, and Slave Schedules.

Ninth Census of the United States, 1870: Craven County, North Carolina, Population Schedule.

Seventh Census of the United States, 1850: Beaufort, Craven, Jones, and New Hanover Counties, North Carolina, Agriculture, Population and Slave Schedules.

Singleton, Henry, Declaration for Pension, April 9, 1898, February 21, 1907, October 8, 1913, July 28, 1924, and January 25, 1929, War Department, Record and Pension Office.

Singleton, Loethe [*sic*], Standard Certificate of Death, January 13, 1926, Bureau of Records of the Department of Health of the City of New York.

Singleton, Maria, Death Certificate, May 15, 1898, Connecticut State Department of Health, Bureau of Vital Statistics.

Singleton, Mary K., Declaration for Widow's Pension, October 15, 1938, War Department, Record and Pension Office.

Singleton, William Henry, and Mary K. Powell, Marriage License, September 2, 1929, Connecticut State Department of Health, Bureau of Vital Statistics.

Tenth Census of the United States, 1880: Craven County, North Carolina, Population Schedule.

Thirteenth Census of the United States, 1910: New Haven County, Connecticut, Population Schedule.

Craven County, North Carolina

Craven County Deeds, Register of Deeds Office, New Bern.

Craven County Marriage Records, Register of Deeds Office, New Bern.

New Bern Town Taxables Records, 1834, 1842, 1845-1846, 1848, 1849, 1859. Original volumes in collection of Tryon Palace Historic Sites and Gardens, New Bern.

North Carolina State Archives, Raleigh, North Carolina

Craven County Census School Reports and Settlements, 1841-1861.

Craven County Cohabitation Records, 1866 (microfilm).

Craven County Estates Records, 1745-1945.

Craven County Marriage Bonds.

Craven County Military Collection, Civil War Collection.

Craven County Miscellaneous Records, Slaves and Free Negroes, 1775-1881.

Craven County Wills, 1748-1911.

Descriptive Books of the Thirty-fifth, Thirty-sixth, and Thirty-seventh Regiments of the United States Colored Troops.

North Carolina Freedman's Savings and Trust Company Records (microfilm).

Secondary Sources

Books and Articles

Andrews, William L. *To Tell A Free Story: The First Century of Afro-American Autobiography, 1760-1865*. Chicago: University of Illinois Press, 1988.

Baker, Osmon C. *A Guidebook in the Administration of the Discipline of the Methodist Episcopal Church*. New York: Carlton and Phillips, 1855.

Barrett, John G. *The Civil War in North Carolina*. Chapel Hill: University of North Carolina Press, 1963.

Benam's Greater New Haven, City Directory and Annual Advertiser. New Haven, Conn.: J. H. Benam.

Berlin, Ira, Joseph P. Reidy, Leslie Rowland, eds. *Freedom: A Documentary History of Emancipation, 1861-1867—Series 2: The Black Military Experience*. Cambridge: Cambridge University Press, 1993.

Blassingame, John W. *The Slave Community: Plantation Life in the Antebellum South*. New York: Oxford University Press, 1979.

Boatner, Mark Mayo, III. *The Civil War Dictionary*. Rev. ed. New York: David McKay Company, 1988.

Brown, William Wells. *The Negro in the American Rebellion.* Annotated by William Edward Farrison. New York: Citadel Press, 1971.

Butterfield, Stephen. *Black Autobiography in America.* Amherst: University of Massachusetts Press, 1974.

Campbell, Robert A. *The Rebellion Register.* Kalamazoo, Mich.: R. A. Campbell, 1866.

Carraway, Dollie C. *South River: A Local History From Turnagain Bay to Adams Creek.* 2d ed. Fayetteville, N.C.: M and L Designs, 1994.

Cecelski, David S. "Abraham Galloway: Wilmington's Lost Prophet and the Origins of Black Radicalism in the South." In *Democracy Betrayed: The Wilmington Race Riot of 1898 and Its Legacy,* edited by David S. Cecelski and Timothy B. Tyson. Chapel Hill: University of North Carolina Press, 1998.

———. "Oldest Living Confederate Chaplain Tells All? Or James B. Avirett and the Rise and Fall of the Richlands." *Southern Cultures* 3 (winter 1997): 5-24.

———. "The Shores of Freedom: The Maritime Underground Railroad in North Carolina, 1800-1861." *North Carolina Historical Review* 71 (April 1994): 174-206.

Clinton, Catherine. *The Plantation Mistress: Woman's World in the Old South.* New York: Pantheon Books, 1982.

Corbitt, David Leroy. *The Formation of North Carolina Counties, 1663-1943.* Raleigh, N.C.: State Department of Archives and History, 1956.

Coyler, Vincent. *A Brief Report of the Services Rendered by the Freed People to the U.S. Army in North Carolina, In the Spring of 1862, After the Battle of New Bern.* New York: Vincent Coyler, 1864.

Directory of Peekskill (New York). Newburgh, N.Y.: Breed Publishing Company, 1905-1908, 1915, 1920, 1924.

Douglass, Frederick. *Narrative of the Life of Frederick Douglass, An American Slave, Written By Himself.* New York: Penguin Classics, 1986.

Dyer, Frederick H. *A Compendium of The War of the Rebellion.* Vol. 3, *Regimental Histories.* New York: Thomas Yoselfhoff, 1959.

Emmerton, James A. *A Record of the Twenty-third Regiment Mass. Vol. Infantry, in the War of the Rebellion, 1861-1865.* Boston, Mass.: William Ware and Company, 1886.

Foster, Francis Smith. *Written By Herself: Literary Production by African American Women, 1746-1892.* Bloomington: Indiana University Press, 1993.

Foster, Richard A. G. "Short History of Varick Memorial African Methodist Episcopal Zion Church New Haven, Conn." *A.M.E. Zion Quarterly Review* 56 (winter 1945-1946): 17-21.

The General Conferences of the Methodist Episcopal Church from 1792-1896. New York: Eaton and Mains, 1900.

Genovese, Eugene D. *Roll, Jordan, Roll: The World the Slaves Made.* New York: Vintage Books, 1976

Greater New Haven City Directory. New Haven, Conn.: Price and Lee, 1904, 1905, 1910, 1920, 1928, 1930-1938.

The History of American Methodism in Three Volumes. Vol.2. New York: Abingdon Press, 1964.

Hood, James W. *One Hundred Years of the African Methodist Episcopal Zion Church.* New York: A.M.E. Zion Book Concern, 1895.

Howell, Peter. *The Life and Travels of Peter Howell, Written By Himself.* New Bern, N.C.: W. H. Mayhew, 1849.

Hubbell, John T., and James W. Geary. *Biographical Dictionary of the Union, Northern Leaders of the Civil War.* Westport, Conn.: Greenwood Press, 1995.

Jacobs, Harriet. *Incidents in the Life of a Slave Girl, Written By Herself.* Edited by Jean Fagan Yellin. Cambridge, Mass.: Harvard University Press, 1987.

Johnson, Guion Griffis. *Ante-Bellum North Carolina: A Social History.* Chapel Hill: University of North Carolina Press, 1937.

Joyner, Charles. *Down By the Riverside: A South Carolina Slave Community.* Urbana: University of Illinois Press, 1984.

Keckley, Elizabeth. *Behind the Scenes, or Thirty Years a Slave and Four Years in the White House.* New York: Oxford University Press, 1988.

Kirwan, Thomas. *Soldiering in North Carolina.* Boston, Mass., 1864.

Litwack, Leon F. *Been in the Storm So Long: The Aftermath of Slavery.* New York: Vintage Books, 1980.

MacLean, Nancy. *Behind the Mask of Chivalry: The Making of the Second Ku Klux Klan.* New York: Oxford University Press, 1994.

Manarin, Louis H., and Weymouth T. Jordan Jr., comps. *North Carolina Troops, 1861-1865: A Roster.* 14 vols. to date. Raleigh: Division of Archives and History, Department of Cultural Resources, 1966-.

Methodist Episcopal Church, Conferences, *Minutes of the Annual Conferences of the Methodist Episcopal Church, South.* Raleigh, N.C.: Methodist Episcopal Conference, published annually for the years 1845-1865.

————. *Minutes of the Annual Conferences.* Raleigh, N.C.: Methodist Episcopal Conference, published annually.

Mitchell, Memory F. "Off to Africa—With Judicial Blessing." *North Carolina Historical Review* 53 (summer 1976): 265-287.

Munjoy Hill Historic Guide. Portland, Maine: Greater Portland Landmarks, 1992.

The National Cyclopædia of American Biography. Vol. 2. New York: James T. White and Company, 1921.

Oakes, James. *The Ruling Race: A History of American Slaveholders.* New York: Alfred A. Knopf, 1982.

Olney, James. "I Was Born: Slave Narratives, Their Status as Auto-biography and as Literature." In *The Slave Narrative*, edited by Charles T. Davis and Henry Louis Gates Jr. New York: Oxford University Press, 1985.

Personal War Sketches of the Admiral Foote Post, No. 17, Grand Army of the Republic. New Haven, Conn., 1890.

Phillips, Ulrich Bonnell. *The Slave Economy of the Old South: Selected Essays in Economic and Social History.* Edited by Eugene D. Genovese. Baton Rouge: Louisiana State University Press, 1968

Portland City Directory. Portland, Maine: Portland Directory Company, 1899-1903.

Powell, William S. *Dictionary of North Carolina Biography.* Vol. 3. Chapel Hill: University of North Carolina Press, 1988.

————. *The North Carolina Gazetteer: A Dictionary of Tar Heel Places.* Chapel Hill: University of North Carolina Press, 1968.

Record of the Service of Connecticut Men in the Army & Navy of the United States During The War of the Rebellion. Hartford, Conn.: Press of the Case, Lockwood, Brainard Company, 1889.

Redkey, Edwin S., ed. *A Grand Army of Black Men: Letters from African American Soldiers in the Union Army, 1861-1865.* New York: Cambridge University Press, 1992.

Reid, Richard. "Raising the African Brigade: Early Black Recruitment in Civil War North Carolina." *North Carolina Historical Review* 70 (July 1993): 266-301.

Sandbeck, Peter B. *The Historic Architecture of New Bern and Craven County, North Carolina.* New Bern, N.C.: Tryon Palace Commission, 1988.

Schweninger, Loren. "John Carruthers Stanly and the Anomaly of Black Slaveholding." *North Carolina Historical Review* 67 (April 1990): 159-192.

Shotwell, R. A. *New Bern Mercantile and Manufacturers' Business Directory and N.C. Farmer's Reference Book*. New Bern, N.C.: W. I. Vestal, 1866.

Sifakis, Stewart. *Who Was Who in the Civil War*. New York: Facts on File Publications, 1988.

Smith, Chester A. *Peekskill, A Friendly Town: Its Historic Sites and Shrines: A Pictorial History of the City From 1654-1952*. Peekskill, N.Y.: Friendly Town Association, 1952.

Stevenson, Brenda E. *Life in Black and White: Family and Community in the Slave South*. New York: Oxford University Press, 1996.

Still, William. *The Underground Railroad: A Record of Facts, Authentic Narratives, Letters, etc., Narrating the Hardships, Hair-Breadth Escapes, and Death Struggles of the Slaves in Their Efforts for Freedom*. Philadelphia: Porter and Coates, 1872.

Tigert, John J., ed. *The Doctrines and Discipline of the Methodist Episcopal Church, South*. Nashville, Tenn.: Barbee and Smith, 1898.

Trowbridge, Francis Bacon. *The Trowbridge Genealogy: History of the Trowbridge Family in America*. New Haven, Conn.: Tuttle, Morehouse and Taylor Company, 1908.

U.S. Bureau of the Census. *Agriculture of the U.S. in 1860, Compiled from the Original Returns of the Eighth Census*. Washington, D.C.: Government Printing Office, 1864.

U.S. Bureau of the Census. *Fourteenth Census of the U.S.* Vol. 1, *Population Number And Distribution of Inhabitants*. Washington, D.C.: Government Printing Office, 1921.

U.S. Bureau of the Census. *Statistical View of the U.S., Compendium to the Seventh Census*. Washington, D.C.: Government Printing Office, 1854.

U.S. Bureau of the Census. *Statistics of the U.S. in 1860, Compiled from the Original Returns and Being the Final Exhibit of the Eighth Census*. Washington, D.C.: Government Printing Office, 1866.

The War of the Rebellion: A Compilation of the Official Records of the Union and Confederate Armies. 70 vols. in 127. Washington, D.C.: Government Printing Office, 1880-1901.

Warner, Robert Austin. *New Haven Negroes: A Social History.* New Haven, Conn.: Yale University Press, 1940.

Watson, Alan D. *A History of New Bern and Craven County.* New Bern: Tryon Palace Commission, 1987.

White, Deborah Gray. *Ar'n't I a Woman? Female Slaves in the Plantation South.* New York: W. W. Norton and Company, 1985.

Wright, R. R. *The Bishops of the African Methodist Episcopal Church.* Nashville, Tenn.: A.M.E. Sunday School Union, 1963.

Newspapers

Highland Democrat (Peekskill, N.Y.).

New Berne Journal.

New Haven Evening Register.

New Haven Journal-Courier.

Interviews

Fitch, Leroy E. Interview by Katherine Mellen Charron. New Haven, Conn. February 11, 1999. Telephone interview by Katherine Mellen Charron. March 1, 1999.

Twyman, Charles. Telephone interview by Katherine Mellen Charron. New Haven, Conn. February 12, 1999.

Vlock, Laurel F. Interview by Katherine Mellen Charron. New Haven, Conn. February 18, 1999.

Index

A

Abbott, W. H., 59

Abolitionism: espoused by Eliza H. Nelson, 10, 43, 84-85; at Garbacon Creek, 8-10; in New Bern, 9, 79; WHS learns of, 85; slaveholders fear, 86; in slave narratives, 21-22

Adams Creek, 13, 80, 87; map of, 4

Adams Creek Methodist Episcopal Church, 88-89

Admiral Foote Post, No. 17, Grand Army of the Republic, 52, 59, 104

African American autobiography, 19-26

African Americans: in Craven County, 3; in the military, 1-2, 10-11, 48-50, 60, 95, 97-98, 101; pictured, following 54; in New Bern, 5, 9, 82; move to New Haven, 26, 101. *See also* Free blacks; Singleton, William Henry; Slaves

African Brigade, 2, 97; pictured, following 54

A.M.E. Zion churches: in New Bern, 26, 58, 95, 100; in New Haven, 26, 59, 95, 99, 100; in Portland, 60, 102

A.M.E. Zion New England Conference, 26, 100

Andrew, James O., 87-88

Andrew, John A., 96-97

Andrew's Chapel (Saint Peter's Church), 26-27, 94, 100; shown on map, following 54

Ayers, Mr. (presiding elder), 12, 45-46, 89

B

Beecher, Henry Ward, 49, 96

Beecher, James Chaplain, 49, 96, 97; pictured, following 54

Best, George W., 75

Betty (WHS's aunt): age of, 83; family of, 14, 63, 68, 75; family of, separated, 15; on slave list, 16

Bill (WHS's uncle) 16, 17, 63, 68, 75

Blackledge, Elizabeth. *See* Singleton, Elizabeth Blackledge
Branch, Lawrence O'B., 57, 92
Brown, John, 9, 23, 43, 56, 85
Brown, William Wells, 99
Buchanan, George W., 52, 60, 104
Burnside, Ambrose E.: captures New Bern, 10, 46, 57, 92; departs North Carolina, 95-96; on Foster's progress, 94; headquarters of, 92; identified, 91; meets with Lincoln, 48-49, 96; pictured, following, 54; at Roanoke Island, 93; on runaway slaves, 92; WHS speaks with, 48

C

Camp meetings, 44, 86-87, 89
Caroline (WHS's cousin): family of, 63, 68, 75; family of, separated, 83-84; on slave list, 16
Clark, Charles C., 90
Clark, George F., 51, 60, 104
Closs, William, 89
Comfort (WHS's grandmother): age of, 76; family of, 14, 63, 68, 75; family of, separated, 15; inherited by Ester E. Nelson, 15, 75; on slave list, 16, 17
Court, John, 83
Craven County: Methodists in, 89; population of, 3, 67, 78-79

D

Delamar, Ennis, 10, 45-46, 74, 89
Delamar, Joseph, 83
Delamar, Stephen, 89
Delamar, William, 89
Dick (WHS's uncle), 14, 16, 63, 75
Dickson, Eleanor (Elinor) Singleton, 65, 71
Dix, John A., 96
Douglass, Frederick, 6, 21, 99
Du Bois, W. E. B., 60

E

Emancipation Proclamation, 49, 57
Evergreen Cemetery (New Haven, Conn.), 28, 61

F

First North Carolina Colored Infantry. *See* Thirty-fifth Regiment, United States Colored Troops
First Regiment, North Carolina Cavalry (Ninth Regiment, North Carolina State Troops), 46, 93
First South Carolina Volunteers, 97
Fitch, Althea E., 63, 102
Fitch, Charles. *See* Fitch, Collins L. (Charles)
Fitch, Collins, Jr., 63, 102

Fitch, Collins L. (Charles), 51, 60, 63, 102

Fitch, George M., 63, 102

Fitch, Harrison B., 63, 102

Fitch, Jerome H., 63, 102

Fitch, Leroy E., 63, 69, 102

Fitch, Lulu Singleton. *See* Singleton, Lulu W.

Fitch, Milton F., 63, 102

Fitch, William S., 63, 102

Foote Street A.M.E. Zion Church (Varick Memorial A.M.E. Zion Church), 59, 61, 99

Foster, John Gray: advances on Kinston, 94; ambivalent about African American troops, 97; appointed military governor, 92; approves classes for African Americans, 101; arms former slaves, 10-11; identified, 91; pictured, following 54; WHS mentions, 46

Frank (slave), 17, 42, 84

Free blacks, 3, 5, 82

Fulford, Joseph, 76

G

Galloway, Abraham, 97-98

Garbacon Creek: abolitionism at, 8-10; absence of black strangers at, 6; agriculture at, 7; becomes part of Carteret County, 72; isolation of, 5; location of, 3; map of, 4; social life at, 8

Garrison, William Lloyd, 9, 23, 43, 86

Gaston House Hotel, 7, 56, 81; shown on map, following 54; pictured, following 54

Grant, Edmund H., 79

Green Memorial A.M.E. Zion Church, 102

H

Hall, Eliza (Eliza Hall Nelson's niece), 72

Hall, Eliza (John H. Nelson's wife). *See* Nelson, Eliza Hall

Hall, John, 84

Hall, John J., 72

Hall, Josephine, 72

Hall, Josephus, 72

Hall, Julia Ann, 72

Hall, Love, 84

Harding, Francis A., 87

Hawks, Ann Singleton, 65, 71

Hinman, Charlotte. See Singleton, Charlotte Hinman.

Honey Hill, Battle of, 58, 98

Hood, James W.: as missionary to New Bern, 26-27, 58, 95, 100; as pastor in New Haven, 26-27, 99, 100; pictured, following 54

Hughes, Isaac M., 82

Hughes and Dudley, 81

Hyman, Mary Nelson. *See* Nelson, Mary C.

Hyman, Samuel, Sr., 64, 83, 90

Hyman, Samuel O., Jr.: death of, 91; enlists, 57, 91; on eve of Civil War, 90; family of, 14, 64; lives at hotel, 56; WHS accompanies, 46; at Wise Forks, 94

J

Jacob (WHS's grandfather): family of, 14, 63, 68, 75; family of, separated, 15; on slave list, 16, 17
Jacobs, Benjamin, 79
Jacobs, Harriet, 18, 78
Jacobs, Mr. (owner of WHS's grandmother), 36-37
Johnson, James Weldon, 24, 60

K

Keckley, Elizabeth, 22
Kinston, N.C., 94
Ku Klux Klan, 24, 51, 60, 61

L

LeBaron, Lillian E., 60, 104
Leggett, Robert, 47, 48, 57, 93, 94
Lincoln, Abraham: reviews troops, 96; WHS hears of, 43; WHS meets, 31, 48-49, 53, 57, 95
Little Egypt, 3, 67
Longstreet, A. B., 88

M

Mason, Francis, 87
Mason, Mehetible N. *See* Nelson, Mehetible "Hettie" Mason
Mennet, O. H., 1
Merrimon United Methodist Church. *See* Adams Creek Methodist Episcopal Church
Methodist Episcopal Church, 55, 87-88, 89, 90
Mitchell, Alexander, 79, 82
Moore, William P., 79, 81-82
Mount Olivet Baptist Church, 104

N

Native Americans, 3, 7
Nelson, Arnest, 63, 75, 90
Nelson, Benjamin F.: death of, 15, 71, 83; family of, 64; inherits slaves, 17, 74
Nelson, Charles, 75
Nelson, Cora L., 64, 84
Nelson, Edward H., 14, 41, 70, 83
Nelson, Eliza Hall: death of, 14, 84; expresses abolitionist views, 10, 42, 84-85; family of, 64, 72; marries, 56, 84; WHS's opinion of, 42, 43
Nelson, Ester E.: family of, 64; inherits slaves, 15, 17, 74, 75, 83; marriage agreement of, 76; marries, 8; resides in New Bern, 15; as widow, 13

Nelson, Francis L., 64, 84

Nelson, Harry V., 64, 75

Nelson, James, 74

Nelson, James F., 87

Nelson, John (ancestor of John S. and John H. Nelson), 7, 74

Nelson, John H.: age of, 83; buys land, 13, 56, 74; confronted with abolitionism, 9-10, 42; description of, 40; as executor, 8, 72; family of, 64; manservant requested of, 90; marries, 14, 43, 56, 84, 85; in New Bern, 5; plantation of, 3, 4, 7-8, 13, 32, 72, 73, 74-75; prohibits slaves from learning to read, 41, 43; public life of, 8, 80; religious activities of, 8, 44, 46, 87; responds to prayer by slave, 46; sells WHS, 8, 15, 20, 33, 39, 40, 55, 56; slaves of, 7-8, 9, 14, 17, 32, 41, 42, 43, 44, 70, 72, 73, 74, 83, 84, 89

Nelson, John S.: buys land, 7; death of, 73; family of, 64; slaves of, 14, 16, 17, 75, 76

Nelson, Josephus, 64, 75, 76

Nelson, Lettice (Singleton), 32; age of, 84; family of, 63, 75; family of, separated, 14-15; inherited by John H. Nelson, 14-15, 74; on Nelson plantation, 7, 55, 84; post-war home of, 50, 51; relationship with

Arnest Nelson, 90, with WHS's father, 18, 19; WHS reunites with, 38; WHS seeks, 37; on slave list, 16, 17

Nelson, Mary C., 17, 64, 74

Nelson, Mehctible "Hettie" Mason, 14, 56, 64, 85

Nelson, Susan J., 64, 84

Nelson, Susan T.: family of, 64; inherits slaves, 15, 17, 74, 84; marries, 8, 84

Nelson, Wiley M.: death of, 56; frees slaves, 9, 44, 56, 86; lives near John H. Nelson, 13, 74; property of, in New Bern, 86; religious activities of, 87

Neuse River, 5

New Bern, N.C.: abolitionism in, 9, 79; African Americans leave, 26, 101; African American soldiers recruited in, 97; African American women in, make flag, 98; A.M.E. Zion church in, 26, 58, 95, 100; battle of, 10, 57, 92; free blacks in, 5, 6-7, 82; health care in, 15; map of, 6, following 54; Methodists in, 89; population of, 36, 78; slave laborers in, 5; slave patrols in, 80, 81; slaves go to, 7, 9, 10, 92; ties with New Haven, Conn., 26, 100-101

New Haven, Conn., 26, 27, 100-101

Nicholson, David B., 89

Nicolas (WHS's uncle): family of, 63, 75; family of, separated, 14, 15; on slave list, 16, 17

Ninth Regiment, North Carolina State Troops. See First Regiment, North Carolina Cavalry.

North Carolina Club, 101

O

Olustee, Battle of, 50, 58, 98-99; pictured, following 54

Open Ground pocosin, 3

Oriental Lodge, F. and A.M. (New Haven, Conn.), 52, 59, 104

P

Parker, Lucy, 100

Payten, Henry, 67

Peed, John, 39, 40

Peed, Josephus, 80-81

Peekskill, N.Y., 36, 51-52, 78

Phillips, Wendell, 9, 24, 43, 86

Pleasant (WHS's aunt): family of, 14, 63, 75; family of, separated, 15; inherited by Ester E. Nelson, 15, 83; on slave list, 16

Poor whites, 40, 43, 81, 85

Powell, Mary. See Singleton, Mary Powell

R

Richardson, George A., 93

Richardson, Major, 47, 93

Rush, Christopher, 100

S

Saint Peter's Church. See Andrew's Chapel

Salter, David, 101

Salter, Dempsey, 101

Second Regiment, North Carolina State Troops, 94

Seymour, T., 99

Singleton, Ann. See Hawks, Ann Singleton

Singleton, Charlotte Hinman: death of, 27, 61, 103; family of, 63; marries WHS, 27, 51, 60, 103

Singleton, Eleanor (Elinor). See Dickson, Eleanor (Elinor) Singleton

Singleton, Elizabeth, 74

Singleton, Elizabeth Blackledge, 65, 71

Singleton, Hardy: age of, 19, 70; family of, 63, 73; father of, 18; on Nelson plantation, 7; post-war home of, 50, 51, 73, 101; recognizes WHS, 38

Singleton, Joseph: age of, 19, 73; family of, 63; father of, 18; on Nelson plantation, 7; post-war home of, 50, 51, 73, 101

Singleton, Lettice. See Nelson, Lettice (Singleton)

Singleton, Lulu W.: birth of, 27, 59; family of, 5, 63, 102; marries, 60; pictured, following 54

Singleton, Maria Wanton: death of, 27, 102; family of, 63; marries, 26, 51, 59

Singleton, Martha, 65, 71

Singleton, Mary Powell, 27, 61, 63, 103

Singleton, Richard B., 65, 71

Singleton, Spyers, 65, 71

Singleton, Thomas S., 18, 65, 65, 71, 81

Singleton, William G.: family of, 63, 65; and Lettice Nelson, 19; residence of, 18, 55, 56, 71; work of, 18, 56

Singleton, William Henry: avoids New Bern, 50-51; birth of, 3, 15, 31, 55, 70, 74; business dealings of, 51, 101; on citizenship, 22, 25; during Civil War, 1-2, 10-11, 46-50, 57, 58, 90, 95, 96, 97; death of, 2, 27, 61, 70; family of, 14, 32, 33, 63; father of, 15, 18-19, 24, 32, 41, 71; on freedom, 49, 52; funeral of, 28, 61; hides from slave patrol, 39, 55; learns to read, 26, 50; marries, 19, 26, 27, 51, 59, 60, 61, 102, 103; master of, 12-14; meets Lincoln, 31, 48-49, 53, 57, 95; moves to New Haven, Conn., 26, 27, 50, 59, 61, 99, 100-101, 103, to New York, N.Y., 27, 51, 60, 103, to Peekskill, N.Y., 27, 51, 60, 103, to Portland, Me., 27, 51, 60, 102; as an orator, 27, 103; physical appearance of, 70; pictured, ii, following 54; political allegiance of, 69; post-war employment of, 27, 50, 51, 52, 59, 60, 100, 103, 104; prohibited from learning to read, 41, 43; punishment of, 14, 31, 35, 41; on slavery, 31, 44; on status of African Americans, 52-53; religious activities of, 27, 50, 51, 52, 59, 60, 99, 102, 104; reunites with mother, 38, 40; runs away, 7, 8, 20, 35-37, 39, 40, 46, 55, 56, 78; selling of, 8, 15, 20, 33-34, 39, 40, 55, 56, 82; tombstone of, pictured, following 54; veterans activities of, 1-2, 27, 52, 59, 61, 104; works at hotel, 7, 40; works on plantation, 40-41; during World War I, 51-52

Singleton, William Henry, *Recollections of My Slavery Days*: in African American autobiographical tradition, 19-26; discrepancies in, 12, 102-103; environment at time of writing and publication of, 24; publication of, 2, 61; obscurity of, 2-3; writing of, 2, 11-12, 19

Slave farms, 34, 77

Slave narratives. *See* African American autobiography

Slave patrols, 38-39, 80

Slaves: aid Union army, 10; amusements of, 44; female, affairs with white males, 18-19; former, aid Union army, 93-94; hiring out of, 5-6, 8, 90; literacy among, 21-22, 43, 44; living conditions of, 32; manumission of, 9, 44, 56, 86; monetary value of, 34, 39, 40, 77; in New Bern, 5, 7, 9, 10, 92; punishment of, 10, 35, 83; religious activities of, 9-10, 44, 45, 90; runaway, 9, 10, 34, 81, 92; separation of families of, 14-15, 33-34, 73-74, 76-77; surnames of, 15, 18, 32-33, 74; work of, 32, 34

Slover, Charles, 79

Slover House, 92; pictured, following 54; shown on map, following 54

Stanly, Alexander H., 15, 64, 75, 76

Stanly, Edward, 101

Stanly, Ester Nelson. See Nelson, Ester E.

Stanly, James G., Jr., 64

Stanly, John C., 18

Stanly, Susan Nelson. *See* Nelson, Susan T.

Stanly House, 92; pictured, following 54; shown on map, following 54

Stevenson, George F., 79

Stowe, Harriet Beecher, 96

T

Thirty-fifth Regiment, United States Colored Troops: appointment of captain in, 98; assignments of, 49-50, 58; Beecher assumes command of, 96; at Olustee, 99; Henry Payten in, 67; WHS serves in, 11, 49-50, 97

Trowbridge, Henry, 50, 59, 100

Trowbridge, Thomas R., 50, 59, 100

U

Underground Railroad, 9, 43

V

Varick, James, 99

Varick Memorial A.M.E. Zion Church. *See* Foote Street A.M.E. Zion Church

W

Wade, Amos, 79

Wanton, Maria. *See* Singleton, Maria Wanton

Washington, Booker T., 22, 99

Wheeler, Mr. (New Bern business-
    man), 51

Wheeler, Mrs. (purchaser of
    WHS), 40

Wheeler, Thomas, 101

White, J. C., 49

White, Josiah C., 98

Wild, Edward A., 58, 97; pictured,
    following 54

Williams, Joseph E., 98

Williams, Sam, 93

Wilmington, N.C., 78

Winthrop, John, 13, 32, 56

Winthrop, John S., 74

Wise Forks, Battle of, 94

Wise Forks, N.C., 47, 93, 94

Woodman, George F., 95

World War I, 25, 60

Wyde, Ira S., 89